He SEEMED Normal...

Mary Gulla

Alazar
PRESS
CARRBORO, NORTH CAROLINA

He Seemed Normal . . .

Text copyright 2024 by Mary Gulla

Printed in Canada

Cover design and production by Jennifer Hill
Edited by Sean Brady Kenniff and Michael Rosenthal

ISBN 978-17336865-8-7
First Edition, 2024

is an imprint of Royal Swan Enterprises, Inc.
201 Orchard Lane, Carrboro, NC 27510
Visit us at www.alazar-press.com

For Michael, thank you for believing in me the most.
You will always be remembered.

"I really love wearing perfume."

Andy Warhol

Contents

One

Cast List (Everyone Except the Misters)

I used to think people could see my anxiety, at least until I played violin in concert as a child. My dad recorded the performance—I didn't recognize the composed person who was supposed to be me. I have always been an anxious person with a learning disability.

To compensate, I've learned one strategy that never fails: When trying something new, ask friends to join in so you can figure it out together. That's how I approached dating and the search for my "Manicorn." These pages are about the dates and the men who made them, in one way or another, unforgettable. And here are the people who are also part of my story.

Crafty used to answer to Mayonesa. We met in high school but became friends several years later. Her car always contained multiple coats and always, for years it seemed, had the music of Cat Power coming from the speakers.

SDH and I met through Crafty, and the three of us became great friends and aggressive daters. Her apartment in Carrboro was referred to as Nut Bush. SDH and I watched the movie *Frances Ha* together. We both loved it so much that we started using "Ahoy Sexy!" as a salutation in all of our messages to each other.

Mike is a former coworker who is always on the lookout for beer and Dairy Queen Blizzards. Somehow received permission to wear shorts at work so he didn't overheat. International rock collector. Giver of sage advice.

Monte is a pharmacy school comrade. Answers to Danger. Most likely to be spotted in a novelty t-shirt.

Megan is my youngest sister (we are 6 years apart). Never pierced her ears. No matter where on the planet, she will run into someone she knows or someone she can trace back to someone she knows.

Katie is my younger sister (we are 19 months apart). Owns hundreds of headscarves. We were dressed alike for so many years that the first Thanksgiving we shopped separately, we showed up in the same long, black velvet skirt from Old Navy.

Lilli is an honorary Gulla sister. Can be seen wearing cardigans year-round. Briefly lived with me, and the first thing she asked was how she could be an active member of the household. Could not have loved her more in that moment.

Bernadette is a pharmacy school comrade. Former roommate. Mother hen of friend group. Drink of choice: sloe gin fizz. I will never forget watching the movie *What Lies Beneath* with her. I was so scared! I asked to sleep in her room. Something I had never asked anyone before or since. She has always felt like home to me.

Julie is a pharmacy school comrade. Former roommate. There once was a spider in our apartment and she put on her shoe before stomping it. Talks slowly and sweetly before cursing and saying the dirtiest thing you've ever heard.

Angry Dave and I met while working at Eckerd Pharmacy when I was an intern. Smells like a dryer sheet. I mentioned once that I would love to see Janet Jackson in concert. Years later, when Janet was touring, he surprised me with a ticket. We have talked over countless meals, and the part where he becomes overly passionate about something is always the best part.

Allyson is a former cubicle mate and coworker. Bonded over mutual love for Hello Kitty and nail stickers. When her beloved dog Princess Chomperz made it on the CNN website, it really felt like anything was possible.

Shannon is a pharmacy school comrade. Planner extraordinaire. Partner in hysterical laughter. Asks how I'm doing constantly, and engages with my answer, every single time. Switches to Norm-from-*Cheers* mode when leaving the house. Puts on sneakers as soon as she wakes up and wears them all day long.

Weiderman is also named Shannon. Had our first pharmacy-school rotation together. The moment we were left alone, she asked if I wanted to head to the cafeteria to split a pack of mini donuts, the ones with powdered sugar, first. Instant BFF.

George is married to Weiderman. Reason I met The Manicorn. First person I ever saw fill up a hand cart at an ABC store (the liquor store in North Carolina). I hadn't even known there were hand carts at the ABC store.

Renee is a former co-worker. Most likely to be seen in a dress with a mini backpack. Magically knows how to plan the perfect last-minute vacation.

Daniel is a tattoo artist in NYC. For 10 years, he always asked why I was getting the tattoo (sometimes sighing before he asked), and never ever forgot to wish me a happy birthday.

Meghan is a tattoo artist in NC. Inks magical images that require little to no healing time. Loves Lucinda Williams (me too) and has even met her: "She is exactly who you think she is."

Peter is a cross between Val Kilmer and Tom Cruise, but with Val Kilmer's height—young Val Kilmer. (I'm not sure exactly when it

3

started, but for years he was my last call every single night. We would go over our daily to do lists. It was always the best part of my day).

Irina bought me my first grown-up leather purse from Banana Republic. The only person I've ever met who eats Turkish delight—like she's in *The Lion, the Witch and the Wardrobe.*

Carmen will make you laugh no matter what is happening. Shockingly thoughtful. Introduced me to Romance, a perfume that remains in my rotation even though Carmen has moved on to the same perfume my little sister Megan and Big Freedia wear.

Mom met my dad in high school. Kept her distance at first because he seemed untrustworthy with a girl's heart. That changed at a dance in her junior year. After a few weeks of dating, she put a note in the sleeve of the Chicago II album she was lending him: "I know it has only been a couple of weeks, but I love you." They married right after graduation from college.

Dad first admired my mother as she played in the clarinet section of the high school band. He played drums. She was out of his league, he thought. That changed at the dance he attended his senior year—they danced, went to his house, missed the last bus, and her Dad had to come and pick her up. Beautiful night, rough ending.

Aunt Pat is Mom's oldest sister. Always drinks white wine with ice cubes. Admits to having a very hard time shimmying. (Peter tried to help her with that during a family gathering. I have a picture of him manually trying to shimmy her shoulders).

Aunt Elaine was my mom's second oldest sister. Godmother. Lover of Chanel No. 5, Thierry Mugler's Angel, and Neil Diamond. (She passed her love of these particular perfumes and Mr. Diamond on to me).

Aunt Polly was married to my mom's only (older) brother. Has the best giggle and uses it constantly. Also, she's a pool shark.

Uncle Ray was married to Aunt Elaine. Always had a toothpick in his mouth. Loved his doorbell. It could play songs I never heard another doorbell play.

Cara was my high school BFF. She just wanted to read. Everything else in life was something in the way of her reading more books. Constantly sleep deprived. Her signature style was cutting the neck out of a t-shirt and then wearing it until it disintegrated.

Bill is a coworker. Pulls me aside without warning to recite a monologue from memory. Can light up a stairwell with his voice. Never fails to make a Hawaiian shirt look good at work on a Friday.

Eugene is a former coworker. Full of analogies. I heard through the work grapevine that he bought his wife Kate Spade shoes for their engagement.

Kristen K. was a pharmacy intern at Eckerd. Brimming with energy. Lived with my sister Katie and I in South Carolina for a period of time while she was in school. I cried when she moved out.

Kristen M. is a former pharmacy technician that I met through Monte (they bonded over Harry Potter). Vegetarian that REALLY loves Taco Bell. She came to town, gifted me the perfect red lipstick color, and then we saw a Warhol Polaroid exhibit that kicked off my raging Warhol obsession.

Heidi is a former coworker who answers to Sparkle. Has a baker's soul trapped in a pharmacist's body.

Thomas is Mister Ring of Fire's twin. On my phone for a decade as "The Iceberg." The funniest person I know, also the meanest.

Katie Wilson is an elementary school friend. We shared most of our after-school activities (dance class and swim team). Her family had pizza every Friday night and I thought it was the best thing ever— she was living the dream.

Holly is my first and only college dorm roommate. When I decided to decorate my side of the dorm with images from magazines, she cut out and pasted just eyes, at least fifty, on her side of the room. Worked out constantly. Once was asked out on a date because a guy liked her "calves."

Brett and I attended the same high school but met through our local Red Cross chapter. Shared my desire to always have a cup of coffee wherever we were. Always working towards making the world a better place, without a watch on.

Sarah was a pharmacy intern in South Carolina. Online dated before me. Married someone she met online. First person to expose me to satellite radio. Took me out for my birthday and we listened to vintage Britney Spears as we drove around downtown Charleston.

Sarah and Curtis. Sarah is a former coworker and Pilates class partner. Curtis is married to Sarah and worked for the same company as my father, IBM. Curtis would meet us at the secret bar in Carrboro on Monday nights. We would drink the best and most potent Manhattans and chat. It was the most fun I have ever had on a Monday. They are also big fans of *A Muppet Family Christmas*.

Justin is married to my chef-sister Katie. Also, a chef. The morning after they moved in with me, I found his laptop in the refrigerator— that's just what he did when it overheated. Once drove a ham cross country. It was delicious.

Dave is married to my sister Megan. Was a contestant on Jeopardy. Most likely to be spotted in something purple.

Brenden is a former Eckerd coworker. Drove a bike taxi in Charleston while figuring out if he wanted to go to law or pharmacy school. I wrote him a recommendation for both but still don't know if he went to either school. Strongly dislikes Coldplay.

Evelyn is also a former Eckerd coworker. Worked 8-hour shift that overlapped with my 12-hour shift. Introduced me to cranberry juice and gin cocktails, and Walmart's sparkly blue (hidden) poinsettias. Makes me feel like I'm part of her actual family. (What an honor that continues to be!)

Monique was my middle school BFF. Smelled like JOOP! Always had perfectly scrunched hair.

Amber was a coworker at Eckerd. Wore a fake engagement ring during her shift because she was hit on so much at the register. We spent a day off making a pilgrimage to Savannah to get tattoos when they were still illegal in the state of South Carolina. It was one of the best days of my life.

Evan was a high school comrade. Dated high school comrade Crafty after high school. Married a woman he met online. (She is practically perfect in every way).

Two

Overture

"Hairy coward!" I screamed, as I slapped the first male who ever asked me if I wanted to "go out". It was the beginning of sixth grade and my first year at a Quaker Friends School. My sisters and I had been enrolled in Catholic school right after I had attended synagogue school for kindergarten, and before we started going to the Quaker School. My Mom had enrolled me in the synagogue school because she'd heard it was the best school in our neighborhood. We are not Jewish. I had never stepped foot in a synagogue or known anything of the Jewish faith. Consequently, one day during Hanukkah, I got into an extensive argument with the other kindergartners. It was the classic Christmas vs. Hanukkah battle. In my corner, it was just me, the Catholic girl named Mary. In the opposing corner was the rest of the class.

I was asked to leave the classroom because I was so upset and causing a disruption. The next day, my teacher took me aside and gave me a wooden jewelry box with my name on it. She said it was a Hanukkah gift and that I couldn't show anyone. I quickly put it in my backpack. My family moved out of that neighborhood just in time for me to start first grade at St. Christopher's.

My parents had met at a Catholic high school, segregated along the gender binary, of course. So that is what they knew—parochial schooling. Our new neighborhood surrounded the church and school, and everyone I knew went there. We attended Mass every Sunday. Decades later, when my godmother passed away, she was buried on the grounds of St. Christopher's. Her funeral was the first time I had stepped foot in the church since I was 12. It looked exactly the same and still smelled like stale incense. I stood in silence with my sister Katie, wanting to cry. It felt like home. I didn't want to leave.

The only time I didn't feel like an outsider during my schooling was at St. Christopher's. I was named after Jesus' mom, after all, and everyone there believed in Santa Claus. However, I have always felt like I was given the wrong name. A lot of other people feel the same way too, I think, which is why I have so many nicknames. On the rare occasion that someone close to me uses my real name, it startles me.

At the pharmaceutical call center where I work, I have to say my name with every call I take, and many of my callers think it is a fake name, like older ladies who don't like my answers to their questions. "Mary," they say, "how convenient to have such a generic name. Everyone there is probably named 'Mary.'"

"Oh, really?" I say. "Your name is Dolores? I have spoken with no less than five women named Dolores already today. I haven't spoken with a single Mary. Dolores seems to be a dime a dozen name!" I didn't actually say that to poor, ignorant Dolores, but I thought it in my head.

Mary is a family name. I can always tell when someone has a Mary in their life that they love because they say my name slower. Callers will pause and say, "My grandmother is named Mary," or sometimes it's their wife, and then I know no matter how they feel about my answers to their inquiry, they can't possibly get upset or mad at grandma's namesake.

My mother valued her children's education—almost as much as our appearances—and so much so, that when my fifth-grade teacher pronounced the name of the river Danube, "*Dan-you-bee*," she decided it was time to switch schools, again. That is how my sisters and I ended up at a Quaker Friends School.

The year of The Slap, I rode the bus with the most popular girl in my grade. "You have to do it at lunch, in front of everyone," she instructed. Rachel had been dating, so she knew what a guy would hate: a scene. "This is what he gets for lying about you. He deserves it," she assured me.

The hairy coward had asked me if I wanted to "go out with him" after he'd pulled me into our classmates' dark dining room at a house party. Even though I didn't like him and all his dark body hair (I was 11), I said yes. As soon as I said yes, I felt nauseous. I wanted out.

Less than 24 hours later, I called him from my father's downstairs office phone and broke up with him. "I don't want to go out with you anymore!" I didn't know what else to say, so I just hung up without giving him a chance to talk. It was over. I sat back in my Dad's leather work chair and instantly felt less nauseated.

When we'd gone back to school Monday morning, I had found out he was telling everyone that he had broken up with me. I didn't just want to clear things up, I wanted revenge, which is why I angrily consulted my bus-mate Rachel.

I hit the hairy coward so hard that he had a red handprint on his face for the entire period that followed.

In 7th grade, my math teacher confessed to me that he had asked the headmaster to tell him one thing about each of his students. My thing was what I had done in the cafeteria. He could not believe it. It didn't fit with who he saw in his class every day. (That teacher also confessed to me that I reminded him of his girlfriend, so much so that he listed off all our similarities. Apparently, she also owned a gold pin of a cat looking in a mirror - it was a gift, I am not a cat person. He concluded the lecture by saying I was going to marry someone exactly like him. Spoiler alert: I did not. But as expected, he ended up marrying his girlfriend and having four kids. To this day, they are still happily married, according to social media).

I could not believe that the headmaster of the school knew about The Slap, and yet I never got in trouble. However, my mother found out when one of my sixth-grade frenemies decided to tell her while we were giving said frenemy a ride home. I pleaded with my eyes from the front seat, but she just smiled and said, "I still can't believe what you did today!" My mother took the bait. She was livid.

"Mary Elizabeth Gulla, I sent you to a Quaker school! Pacifism is a cornerstone of their religion, and you hit someone?!" She never asked me why. She just yelled and drove like a mad woman all the way home. Thankfully, once she drove it out of her system, I was never punished for it and it was never spoken of again. I felt like I had gotten away with something, until I realized I had marked myself as undatable for the rest of middle school. This is how my dating life started and then promptly stalled out.

Turns out, Rachel was right. But, what boys hate even more than a scene, is being assaulted. Go figure. Because of The Slap, as well as my name-brandless-wardrobe, underdeveloped chest, and no makeup uncuteness—no boys were interested in me.

I started high school a month before turning 14 and just after moving from Pennsylvania to North Carolina. For my birthday, my mother's present to me was an hour-long session with her current "advisor." My mom didn't call her a psychic, she called her Roberta. I did not know what to call Roberta, but from my 14-year-old perspective, she seemed to have psychic-ish abilities. She was also a minister of this church I had never heard of called The International Church of Ageless Wisdom. It felt like my mom was on the phone with her a lot. Roberta lived in Pennsylvania, and there was one day I was summoned to my mom's bedroom while she was on the phone with her. Roberta had told her to get me, specifically, and then handed me the receiver. I was annoyed because I was torn away from my mountain of homework. Mom had always suffered from migraines and I knew she had one that day, so I didn't give her a hard time. Roberta told me to put my hands over my mother's head. I put the phone down and did as she instructed. Roberta began to chant something incomprehensible. All of a sudden, my hands started to radiate heat. It didn't last long, and then Roberta said not to touch the phone and to ask my mother to take the receiver. Then I had to go wash my hands, being careful not to touch anything on the way to the sink, as instructed. I washed my hands and the burning went away. I rejoined Mom on the side of her bed to ask her what the hell just happened. She said that she felt this whooshing in her head and then the headache just leapt through the top of her head and into my hands. That is why I could not touch anything, otherwise I would have *transferred* the headache. What?!

Later, my mom asked me if I had felt anything. I told her my hands slowly became hotter and then they started to burn. "So, where did it go, the headache, down the drain?" I asked, as if her migraine was an errant contact lens. My mom just threw up her hands, "Who knows, Honey!" She was just happy to be rid of the migraine. I shook my head and went back to my studies. I didn't have time for ... this.

In addition to moving migraines out of people's heads over the phone, Roberta touted this thing called a "Blueprint for a Loving Lifetime Mate." First, you had to follow Roberta's belief structure. One of the things she believed was that the universe was alive and always listening. So, in order to find your loving lifetime mate, you had to give the universe your shopping list for what you wanted in one. You had to write it down, say it out loud, and "Keep it in your Bible."

I went to the Dollar Tree and bought a Bible specifically to hold my list. The first list I made was three and a quarter pages, typed and single spaced—and I wondered why I never had a boyfriend in high school. I still have two versions of the typed-up list but not my Dollar Tree Bible. Some items on my original shopping list include necessities such as, "has okay personal hygiene (showers once in a while), speaks English, is able to read a map, 5'11" or taller, nice hair style, is in good mental health, has found their happiness or at least is interested in finding it, is totally free of any communicable and sexually transmitted diseases, and does not have a drinking problem."

All it took to land the ideal boyfriend was to write a list of requirements and slam it in my $1-bible. Poof! And he would suddenly appear. That is what my mother believed because she didn't know any better, and, so, neither did I. (Thanks Mom!) If Roberta said make a list, you made a list. I think my mother ended up thinking I had followed the instructions wrong. When I would mention bad dates and bad boyfriends, she would tell me to edit my list. It was the list's fault.

I have made many modifications to the list over the years. I went back and crossed out "does not have a drinking problem" and scribbled "unselfish" under "handsome" and "not apathetic or lethargic" under "unmarried". I also added, "is able to protect me and help me be deadly at cocktail parties". Teenage-me would be so disappointed at how many cocktail parties her future actually had in store. Several years, lists, and disappointments later, I had the list pared down to just six things. It hung in my bathroom for years, on a light yellow 3x5 index card.

1. Thoughtful of me and others
2. Is down for anything (easy going)
3. Able to read a map
4. Enjoys movies and live music
5. Drinks coffee and alcohol
6. Accepts my two cocker spaniels, Sophie and Lucy

When I lived in South Carolina (circa 2006) I decided to find my own psychic advisor. She lived down the street from me and had a small sign in her front yard that simply said, "Psychic". That was all the credentials I needed to see. I was not happy with my job and I wanted to find love, which is what I told Sabrina when she asked what had brought me to her. I liked that her methods were way different from my mother's psychic—no readings of past lifetimes over the phone—we were live, in person, with no lists. Nonetheless, I felt like she gave out a lot of homework.

Sabrina would sit me in a dark, cold room (covered with a blanket) and tell me to close my eyes and think about how I wanted my life to be. She sent me off with a crystal flower I had to wear in my bra every day, and instructions to take weekly baths with specified salts and to place a clear container of water under my bed every night. I also had to bring Sabrina a rose and honey among other things. She was cleansing me, apparently, but it felt more like I had taken on a part-time job.

My younger sister Katie—the middle child—would make fun of me and my psychic friend, mercilessly. She would put a jellybean in her bra and tell me to watch her life change as she left the house we shared in West Ashley, just outside downtown Charleston. Katie, a chef, would mock me because it seemed like every time we spoke, I was taking a bath or just got out of a bath or I was telling her I needed to take a bath. To be honest, it was really nice—all the baths and quiet time. I could have gone on like that forever, but the psychic started asking me for excessive amounts of money. She wanted a hundred dollars for every year I had been alive. When I told her I didn't have it, she looked me in the eye and said, "The spirits told me that you do."

Well, the spirits were right, but that's when I stopped going to see Sabrina. I blamed it on the fake Louis Vuitton bag I was carrying around all the time. I walked into a thrift store and it was hanging from the ceiling. I asked the woman behind the counter if it was real and she responded, "Why do you think it's hanging from the ceiling?" Fair enough. I was convinced.

Without knowing, at all, how much a real Louis Vuitton bag should cost, I bought it for $250. One of the handles was coming apart, so I gave it to my youngest sister Megan who was living in New York City at the time. She would get it fixed. The guy fixing it told her it was not real. But he repaired the handle, and it looked real to me, so I continued carrying it. It was tall and skinny, the perfect size to fit my magazines. Anyway, I think Sabrina thought it was real too and that I must be rich. Even without giving her all my money, I ended up exactly where I wanted to be, eventually. Sabrina would always tell me not to worry because her work was guaranteed, but I am not sure I'd give her all the credit.

During the waning days of summer 2008, *The New Yorker* magazine published an interview with Marc Jacobs entitled, "Enchanted: The Transformation of Marc Jacobs." During the interview he was glancing at the word perfect tattooed on his right wrist. Interviewer Ariel Levy asked what it meant and why he was looking at it. He explained one of the things he was ruminating on in rehab, " ... we all have a choice in how to look at things, and when things don't go the way I like, I tend to think they're a problem. Well, you can look at something as a problem, or look at it as a learning experience or opportunity for growth, or whatever ... Everything happens for a reason—and is perfect—and you will benefit from it even if you can't see the benefit [in the moment]."

EVERYTHING about this made sense—to me. It clicked in my head. I instantly found this motto, philosophy, outlook—or whatever— calming. Knowing about this idea of *perfection* was an epiphany. It's the reason I love magazines, aside from the perfume samples.

I had a silver bracelet made that said *perfect*, and it was beautiful, but so delicate that it kept breaking. I kept a little baggie in my purse with pink and purple jewelry pliers and extra jump rings, which are just these little metal rings that I could add, open, or close with the pliers to temporarily keep the *perfect* bracelet on my wrist. I was ready for repairs as soon as the bracelet broke. I needed to see that perfect inscription.

Then I lost it, so I had another *perfect* bracelet made. This time I made sure it was a sturdy bangle bracelet and had *perfect* engraved into the side. The second *perfect* bracelet was a major challenge to get on and off my wrist. I had measured my wrist to get the correct size of bracelet, so why was it so fussy? Initially, I panicked and thought my mother had been right when she warned that cracking my knuckles would cause them to swell, permanently. Once I calmed down and slipped the bangle on, passed my knuckles, I remembered that I had Googled the knuckle-cracking thing and found out that it is not true. This particular bangle just had no give and I may have ordered one size too small--chalk it up to human error.

Of course, soon after having the second bangle made, the first one turned up, flying out of my sheets as I was making my bed one morning. Yes, I even wore the *perfect* bracelet to sleep. I doubled up and wore two *perfect* bracelets until my friend Kristen M went through a breakup that completely caught her off guard.

One night, when I was visiting Kristen M—we were sitting on her bed talking and I was watching her cry, trying not to cry myself—I decided, out of desperation, to take a chance and explain the Marc Jacobs-inspired theory behind the *perfect* bangles. At the end of my speech, I gave her the second *perfect* bracelet.

Soon after she started wearing the *perfect* bangle, Kristen met the man she would marry. To this day, she told me she has never taken it off, not even for showers. That may reflect how difficult it is to take off. Anyway, I was back to wearing the original *perfect* bracelet and performing its almost daily required maintenance so I didn't lose it again.

There came a day when I was tired of living with the fear of losing the *perfect* bracelet and decided it had been a part of my wrist for so long that I needed it there permanently. It was time for the *perfect* tattoo.

My sister Katie thought it was stupid. When she got engaged and started planning her wedding, she started having panic attacks for the first time in her life. I was there for one that kicked in while she was supposed to be trying on wedding dresses with our mother. My mom and I were patiently waiting for her to come out with a wedding dress on, when the lady helping her came out instead and said Katie needed a moment.

I went to check on her and there she was sitting on a stool in a pink silk robe with her head down, gripping a glass of water, looking like a defeated prizefighter.

My sister runs marathons. Unlike me, she can't wait to stick up for herself or for the people she cares about (she has been sticking up for me my entire life). Katie is a restaurant owner and a chef. She is a tough cookie. We are 19 months apart, although everyone thinks she is the older sister. I am, in fact, the eldest. I had never in my life seen her like this. I was panicking, but I wanted to make her laugh because that is what she would do for me. "What the hell is the holdup? You just have to throw on some fancy ass wedding dresses? You look like you just lost the big fight."

She did not smile and eventually managed to croak out that she thought she was having a panic attack, so I sat with her, and when she could talk, I asked her what calmed her down and she said, Justin, her fiancé. After that, I had a bracelet made with his name on it, so she could look at it a million times a day, if needed. Of course, it didn't stop her panic attacks, but I would catch her glancing at it from time to time and it made me smile.

But, if the beginning of the wedding process could do this to my sister, what in the world would it do to me? I filed this moment away under, "reasons to never get married".

I have had just a few panic attacks in my life. The first one occurred before I started high school in North Carolina. For months, I had such bad insomnia that I would get jealous when I saw people sleeping in TV commercials. Initially thinking they would put me to sleep, I grabbed one of my sister Megan's Boxcar Children's books and ended up reading the entire thing. It became my ritual to grab a different book from the series each night in the hopes that it would put me to sleep. I ended up reading entire books instead of sleeping. It was baffling; those books were just not that compelling. The insomnia unceremoniously ended when we moved to North Carolina. I was so relieved to be able to sleep again, it almost didn't matter that my anxiety and panic attacks were intensifying.

My best friend at the time, Monique, was sleeping over when my first panic attack ever came out of nowhere, as they do. We were talking and all of a sudden, my heart started racing and I could not breathe. I was sweating and I had no idea what was happening. I irrationally thought I must have taken too many Excedrin. Even before pharmacy school, I respected drugs and all of their directions and warnings. I knew I only had taken two, but I walked downstairs and grabbed the bottle and stared at the instructions while my heart was pounding. I grabbed some water and went back upstairs and sat on the floor of my tiny bedroom with my back against the dresser.

Monique stared at me. What was happening? I had no answers. Monique and I had gone to the mall the weekend before. Out of the blue I had started crying while I was eating a cheesesteak in the food court. I didn't want to talk about why I was crying. We knew why.

I was leaving the only place I had ever known and a friend that I loved. There was no need to talk about it—it was happening. The thought of possibly going through such an upheaval again, just to say, "I do," did not appeal to me. I would rather just skip all the heart racing, sleepless nights, and uncontrollable crying and go directly to living happily ever after.

My good friend Monte introduced me to the term "Manicorn." She said the reason we were both still single was that we were looking for our Manicorns—and that takes time. Monte has a stool in her kitchen that is from her debutante ball. She is petite (her nickname in pharmacy school was "TOS," aka Tits On a Stick) with long hair that when put up in hot rollers, bounces perfectly behind her when she walks. Monte is equal parts funny, smart, and kind. She knows her worth. We stood firm in our shared belief that if there is one thing you need to be picky about, it is who you will spend the rest of your life with. Settling is not an option and compromise is a dirty word.

When I was a pharmacy intern at Eckerd in Chapel Hill, North Carolina, a retired P.E. teacher from New York, Mr. Rosenberg, came in almost every day. He was always balancing out his complaints with words of wisdom. I would just smile, nod, and say, "Have a good day!"

After three years of this, there was one day when he asked me to meet him in an aisle and said, "I know you don't listen to a lot of what I tell you, which is why I brought you out here to aisle 8".

He looked me in the eyes and said please remember this: "There is nothing worse than a bad marriage." I have no idea why he imparted these words to me in aisle 8. I was busy and he was not my only, ahem, eccentric customer. It was a strange, intense, and anxiety-inducing encounter. I will never forget it.

I have always been an anxious person. I have bitten my nails for as long as I can remember. I had a bleeding ulcer by the end of my first year in high school.

For the most part, I guess I keep it contained, but I'm always on the lookout for ways to calm myself down. What works changes over time. For example, during college, I listened to the song "Pull the Wool" from the *Yeah, It's That Easy* album by G. Love and Special Sauce every single night to fall asleep. I will spare you the lengthy list of everything that I have tried to fall asleep. Now, I just look at my wrist and instantly calm down.

The *perfect* tattoo helped me get through my Manicorn search, as did my online dating cohorts Crafty and Super Dirty Hutch (SDH). We came up with our nicknames after seeing Guy Ritchie's movie *RocknRolla*, where the main characters all went by these evocative aliases—One Two, Mumbles, Handsome Bob, and the rest of "The Wild Bunch". Crafty, SDH, and I had just seen *RocknRolla* and, as we made our way down the street to a bar, we fell silent for a spell and realized we were still making a lot of noise because we were all wearing boots. That evening we named ourselves "The Click Clacks". They call me Produx because I always have tons of products stuffed in my purse, car, work cubicle, house …

I strive to be prepared. It is the Philadelphia Camp Fire Girl in me (Think: Girl Scouts, but I don't ever remember doing any outdoor activities). It was perfect for the Northeast Philly moms that ran it (Think Beverly Goldberg, *the smother*, in the sitcom "The Goldbergs".)

My mother is whatever you call the opposite of a *smother,* but she did use hot rollers to curl her hair every day. I don't remember a day without us all in the car and her wondering out loud, "Did I unplug my curlers?!" Growing up, I never saw her without her hair curled and her jewelry on. She had a period of time where she permed her hair and got acrylic nails, like a lot of the other 80's Moms, but that didn't last long. My mother had her own style. She almost always wore a scarf and often she had a dress on that went past her knees. She was always covered up and dressed up. I don't remember her in jeans until I was in college. She always had makeup in her bathroom, but I don't remember her wearing much. She wore Paloma Picasso perfume from this beautiful, delicate round bottle with frosted glass surrounding clear glass. The perfume was only dabbed on when she went out to classical music concerts with my father. I loved the way it smelled. Although I have never worn it myself, this was my gateway perfume. I wanted to smell that fancy all the time.

All that is left from my time as a Camp Fire Girl is a little red vest with a bunch of patches on it, and my inability to leave home without a collapsible fly swatter, travel rain poncho, pack of seasonally appropriate travel tissues, and a mini fan that plugs into my iPhone, among many, many other things. I guess I have replaced these patches with my tattoos. I am still collecting them as permanent reminders of my adventures, "ah-ha" moments, and accomplishments, no matter how small.

If you are ever suffering from a headache, need a band-aid, or need to put your hair in a ponytail, or have something stuck in your teeth, I am here to dive into my Mary Poppins purse and help. I am pulling these dating stories out of my giant purse in the hopes one of them is the band-aid, ponytail holder, piece of floss, tissue to throw away your gum in, or whatever you need to find your "perfect …"

Three

Mister Ghost

Chapel Hill, NC circa 2000

He was trying to have a romantic relationship with my college roommate, but she wasn't interested. Instead, he became my first boyfriend—the only boyfriend I ever had before embarking on my online dating err... experiments.

Mister Ghost was doing anything he could to get out of the friendzone with my roomie Holly. They were running together on a regular basis and then he asked her to be his date for a rugby dinner. Holly came home that night outraged that he had tried to kiss her. Nonetheless, they continued going on runs together.

I met Mister Ghost when Holly asked him to come to our dorm room and fix her computer. It was my first year of pharmacy school at The University of North Carolina at Chapel Hill, so I was sitting at my desk on the opposite side of the room, desperately trying to figure out some pharmaceutical calculations. I hadn't even noticed he was there, until, from across the room, he yelled: "Who are you?" Not, "What's your name?" Or, "Hi, I'm Mister Ghost." But, "Who are you?" He was different.

"Mary," I said quickly and got back to work. I could feel him looking at me. Perhaps he was waiting for me to ask him about him, but he was there for my roommate–not me.

I was graced with the task of dropping him off at rugby practice, somehow, and we engaged in a more in-depth conversation on the way to the old silver Volvo my sister and I were sharing. He asked a second question: "Is it bulletproof?" while pointing at my large, black, overstuffed, crossbody Esprit messenger bag. Bulletproof?

The bag contained all the things I needed immediate access to at all times, such as Wrigley's Winterfresh full-sugar chewing gum. It was a dark day when I had to give up that gum. My sister Katie and I both loved it and both had to give it up. I was spending a lot of time at the dentist and I think he was getting as tired of seeing me as I was of seeing him. He was trying to get to the bottom of things when I finally told him about my beloved blue gum. He yelled at me: "What do you think is going to happen to your teeth if you are chewing non-sugar-free gum all day?!" He was scary and correct.

After trying several sugar-free options, I switched to Trident Splash Peppermint Swirl, aka Christmas gum, as my sister Katie calls it. There are a lot of peppermint things when Christmas comes around and, being born Catholic, I was raised to love Christmas.

In Catholic School, we were told that we could not read books for fun. If we had to read something, it should be our textbooks. Can you imagine? I am not a fast reader, but I am always reading something. Besides the library, my main supplier of books back in the day was *Scholastic* (if you know, you know). Mom would fill out the newspaper-thin "book fair" order sheet and write a check. Then the books would magically appear on my little desk at school. The text-books-only mandate motivated me to be sneaky with my reading for pleasure. I always had a *Nancy Drew* or *Sweet Valley High* paperback stuffed in my backpack.

I spent most nights reading in the dark because I shared a room with my sister Katie. When I was in high school, there was a used bookstore in Carrboro called Nice Price Books (they also had movies, CDs, records and other items, but mostly books), and I would go there when I had money and randomly pick one book and one CD—something I had never heard or read before. My picks were based on whatever caught my eye, like a crazy name or interesting artwork on the cover. This is how I acquired *The World According to Garp* by John Irving. I carried it around for almost a year because I could not get into it, but I just knew the day would come when I would be suddenly enthralled. I kept trying. I am not easily deterred. I hadn't realized how silly this sounded until my friend and coworker, Carmen, commented that the book must be *really* good. It took me a minute to realize what book she was referring to.

"You carry it around with you everywhere," she gently pointed out, as if I somehow hadn't realized it (I hadn't). When I confessed, I had not really started it, she laughed and shook her head. I did finally get into it, shutting the door one day, flopping on my bed with a giant cup of coffee. I did love it. I knew it!

Aside from reading, my other obsession is make-up. I think it started in 4th or 5th grade. I would beg for makeup and my mother always had the same response, "Do you know why the nuns have such nice skin?" I was still in Catholic School and I did not really covet the complexion of any of the nuns. The one nun who was somewhat approachable only liked to talk to me about her love of M&Ms. She was the only nun who seemed somewhat happy, but I worried about her laser-focus on M&Ms. I tried to explain my concern to my mother but she wasn't listening and answered her own question, "It is because they do not wear makeup." To me, that was not a compelling argument.

Eventually my father brought home a pale peach blush and a light pink CoverGirl LipSlick. These items ignited my love of makeup. LipSlicks are training wheels for real lipstick, but I didn't even bother getting to know other brands. I am a loyal person, so I wore CoverGirl lip slicks for years, until they stopped making them.

In middle school as you know, I rode the bus with who I thought was the most popular girl in our class, Rachel. I couldn't believe my good luck! I am sure she cursed her bad luck every day, but it was the bus route. We developed a relationship on the bus, talking the entire time, but we never spoke at school. Rach (something I never called her) was my window into what I could only label as "popular girl problems". She spoke to me constantly about boyfriend issues and her love of heavy metal, two things I knew nothing about. She became my lip slicks supplier. Rach was an only child and it felt like her mom was constantly taking her shopping. I would give her money and she would buy the lip slicks and hand them off to me on the bus. I didn't have a lot of money. What I did have, went to lip slicks and candy. Eventually, the number of products I needed grew exponentially. It started with my three contraband essentials: gum, LipSlick, and a book. My holy trinity. I had my bag over my shoulder at all times, like a security blanket. It was my woobie which gradually became my conversation starter/armor/bag of tricks masquerading as a sensible carryall.

At 17, I retired the bag that I had carried for my last year of high school. It was a large and very shiny, hot pink pleather tote bag. It received attention from some of the popular girls in school, which caused me a lot of anxiety. These girls, who I admired from afar, would approach me like we were old friends, and ask questions about my bag. I switched to a bag I thought no one would comment on, and no one had, until this guy, Mister Ghost.

"Bulletproof?" he asked, deadpan. At this point the bag felt like it was just another part of my body, so It took me a minute to realize what he was referring to. I found him *not* rude but refreshing. He was ... different. With that question he woke me up, like coffee, and it was time to play. I looked him dead in the eye, smiled, and said, "Of course."

He did not smile back. I would learn later his smiles had to be earned, but it was worth it. I was constantly trying and sometimes succeeding to get him to smile. He smiled like a little boy. His entire face conspired, his eyes shone bright, and his head cocked back a bit. Another childlike quality that had both surprised and endeared

26

him to me is that he said "bye-bye" when ending a phone call. No matter what we were talking about, his "bye-bye" never failed to make me smile. He told me he had a friend he would like to set me up with. Since it was for a show at the Cat's Cradle and he would be there with my roommate, I agreed.

I sat on a couch at the back of the concert venue listening to his friend go on and on about... Well, he just went on and on. A surefire way to get me to tune out almost immediately is to explain the mundane details of your job or if you talk sports. All sports. And this dude was an overachiever. My parents never watched or spoke about sports, at all. Not only is "sports talk" a foreign language to me, but no matter how much you explain it, I do not get it. Most of all, I am not interested. My coworker Mike would say that "in sports, ignorance is total bliss". Mike loves baseball, that is his sport. Mike would tell me that he even thinks better during baseball season. He would always want to talk baseball to me at work and I would listen and he would explain. But I had to remind him, it was part of my black hole—sports and classic rock.

Occasionally, I would look across the back room and catch Mister Ghost trying to determine if I was having a good time. Every time our eyes met, mine were rolling and he would smile, briefly. I finally got away from his friend by saying I had to powder my nose. When I came back, I talked to Mister Ghost instead of his friend. He said he felt bad that his matchmaking skills were off and that I was having a bad time. He bought me a beer.

Although I was grateful for the beer, I was not yet 21 and so my hand was stamped with a large black lightning strike. I hadn't realized there was security staff in the crowd looking for stamped people drinking. I thought I was safe amongst the smoke and concert goers. Then, just a few sips into the free and forbidden Yuengling, it was suddenly ripped from my hand and I was thrown out.

It all happened so fast and without words. I couldn't believe it. I had never been thrown out of anywhere before and I didn't know what to do because I wasn't sure if anyone I came with saw it happen. I sat on the curb, as you do, and waited for the show to finish. Luckily, I didn't have long to wait.

Mister Ghost apologized. He had no idea I wasn't 21 and felt bad for both my unsuccessful date and unexpected ejection. He wanted to make it up to me by taking me out. Looking back, it might have all been an elaborate scheme, but it worked. We went out on our first date, which ended up making the campus paper.

Mister Ghost and I went to the student union to bowl. At that time, I had no extra money for date clothes. I wore my gray, wool Old Navy work pants, which I paired with a thrifted polyester, short-sleeved, white shirt with light blue stars, and black platform slides. And, of course, my giant *bulletproof* bag was slung across my shoulders. My makeup at that time consisted of Covergirl Disco Ball eyeshadow, applied liberally around my eyelids and above, always with some vanilla Lip Smackers lip gloss. This was me getting as dressed up as I possibly could. It was the fullest expression of my fashion sense and resources. "Are you wearing pajamas on our first date?" he asked. I laughed it off.

The Honors Advisory Board was also bowling. A reporter from *The Daily Tar Heel* covered the event and when Mister Ghost was approached and asked about his role in the group, he gave a fake name and major. He told the budding journalist that he was "chairman of the advisory board". The next day, on the front page of *The Daily Tar Heel* was an action shot of him bowling under the pseudonym Ward Zimmerman. Mister Ghost was proving to be amusing, but I wasn't sure if I liked him, liked him. Was he even cute? Did that really matter? I had no idea.

Mister Ghost lived down the street from my dormitory, in a dorm with three other guys. One of them was his best friend who was one of the people who played Ramses, the school mascot.

During a rare snowstorm, we had participated in a giant snowball fight that had spontaneously erupted outside his dorm.

"Well, are you going to date this guy?" asked Angry Dave, the pharmacist I was working with at Eckerd that day.

"You know that Dido song where she says something about the person who gave her the best day of her life, handing her a towel, but all she sees is the person? Well, he handed me a towel after our snowball fight and all I saw was that towel," I replied as Angry Dave smiled and shook his head.

The first time Mister Ghost spent the night in my dorm room, we watched the movie *Run Lola Run,* talked, and just hung out. In the middle of the night, someone decided to dry their sneakers in the oven, setting off the fire alarm. Then we were outside in our regular clothes, slightly disheveled, while everybody else was wearing their pajamas. I looked over to see friends shaking their heads at me and laughing. We were busted. I felt like he was bringing me into this college life, like this is what it was supposed to feel like. It was exciting.

I had an extremely limited friend group for most of high school, as well as a bleeding ulcer by the end of my freshman year. My high school life consisted of me studying and playing the violin. During my meager free time, I volunteered at the Teen AIDS Hotline which was only open Friday and Saturday nights until midnight. I spent weekends locked in an old Red Cross Building, taking calls from other teenagers about sex and their sex lives. I drove myself to senior prom in the 1986 Honda Accord my sister and I shared. I wore a vintage sequin dress, using its belt as a headband. I had found the dress at a local thrift store with my extremely limited friend group named Cara. We met up at the prom with a member of Cara's own limited friend group, Sion, and had a great night.

Mister Ghost knew which bars had back doors that no one was watching, and places that had elevators to bypass the bouncers or that just didn't check IDs. He had it all mapped out. Even underage, I could be where he was. Except, it seemed, he didn't want me there.

During the first and only rugby party I accompanied Mister Ghost to, he disappeared as soon as we walked in the door. It was another occasion when I wasn't appropriately dressed. I had on faux, black, army-style ankle boots, jeans, and a light blue button-down shirt with a brown wool sweater over it. The other girls had on cute, tight outfits with full makeup and hair. They all seemed to be giving me the once over. Ugh.

In my experience, women who give you the up-and-down, toe-to-hair glance only cause trouble. If you spot them, steer clear. I didn't know them or anyone else at the party.

I looked down at my sensible boots, collected my thoughts, and instead of leaving or running to Mister Ghost, I had an epiphany: Even if I am "with" someone, I am all that I have, and so I need to be OK with who I am, no matter where I am.

They were not cute, but they were such good boots—versatile, comfortable, and the perfect light-but-still-chunky heel. They made me taller than Mister Ghost, which I liked. Between you and me, I always feel most comfortable when I am taller than the man I am with.

I grabbed a drink and sat down on a couch with some of the guys, thinking they would either include me or ignore me, but either way I was away from the girls.

I thought maybe Mister Ghost was testing me to see if I could be on my own at parties and not glued to his side. He was a fan of tests and I never really knew with him what was a test and what was not. This felt like a sink-or-swim situation and judging from the look on his face at the end of the evening, he was surprised to find me sitting around with a bunch of his teammates, swapping stories. I was surprised too. It wasn't terrible. Mister Ghost had inadvertently given me the gift of self-confidence. Mister Manicorn, whom I'll meet much later in this story, but will introduce you to now, is also a fan of dropping me at gatherings of his friends—like a baby on her first day at Aqua-Tots. Now it doesn't bother me, but it can take me time to get my swim legs, like at a rehearsal dinner for one of Mister Manicorn's friends.

He had told me not to get too dressed up, we were eating pizza. We got to the rehearsal dinner and it was outside at this beautiful vineyard. I watched other guests arrive and I became more and more upset. These women were in gowns, complete with heels, makeup, and tiny jeweled purses. I was in all GAP with jeans, a white button down, and a blue blazer holding a taco wristlet. It was my attempt at being California chic.

I was standing there, cursing my taco wristlet (which, by the way, is exactly what you are thinking: a wristlet shaped like a taco, made by Betsy Johnson), when two men in pastel suits approached me and said they were just admiring my taco wristlet. I confessed that I had been cursing it. I started waving the wristlet around saying, "LOOK at these women!" (Real quick: I would like to mention that Betsy Johnson also makes a hoagie, champagne bottle, and glittering pizza slice wristlets. I have purchased them all. They are excellent conversation starters). These friendly pastel men asked me if I knew anyone else at the wedding and I said I did not and they said they didn't either. So, it was settled, we would hang out together.

Turns out they were married to each other and one of them had worked with the bride in another life. We sat at the end of a loooooong dinner table, not able to see or hear the bridal party. Delicious brick oven pizza just kept appearing in front of our little group. Arriving late to the dinner were the groom's friends from college who were also informally dressed, think flip- flop casual. This made my taco wristlet look a little fancier, and they were talkative in a way that made it clear they had known each other forever. Their banter was inclusive and hilarious. My stomach hurt from laughing. Eventually, Manicorn made his way down the table too to look for me and when he saw me, he gave me a similar, Mister Ghost-style look of surprise. He sat down with me, with us. Then after all the speeches, the groom came to the end of the table to see who the hell was making all that noise.

Back to Mister Ghost! (We'll press pause on Mister Manicorn, but at least now you've met). Pleasures by Estée Lauder was my preferred perfume when Mister Ghost and I started dating, but I didn't wear it all the time because I wanted/needed to make the bottle last. A lady in my parent's neighborhood that I babysat for in high school wore it, and I fell in love with the scent that lingered for hours after she left. I asked for it for my birthday and I would spritz it on occasionally, when I knew I would be hanging out with Mister Ghost, but he never commented on it until I had not used it for a while. I had sprayed it on my itchy, brown, wool, oversized sweater because I wore it all the time and never washed it. Then one night, I sat next to him in his dorm room and he buried his head in my sweater, just smelling me. He commented that I had not smelled like that in a while. So, without a compliment, I knew that he liked the way I smelled.

We would watch a lot of movies in his dorm room, just the two of us, even though he had two roommates. He was trying to figure out the perfect movie to bring us closer together, physically. We watched *Fight Club.* At the end, I stood up to leave and he grabbed my hand and pointed to the screen as the credits rolled and said, "See, it was a love story!" The two of us stood, holding hands, watching the credits. It was ridiculous. What was happening? This was not romantic.

"I guess you can make any story a love story then," I said, as I was leaving.

Another night we watched *The Hand that Rocks the Cradle*. If he was thinking a thriller would bring us closer together, then it backfired. I could not shut up about her inhaler technique. As you know, I was in pharmacy school at the time and I was not able to suspend reality and just enjoy the movie. I became so frustrated with the actress and her piss poor portrayal of an asthmatic, that I was yelling at the screen every time she picked up the inhaler. In my defense, her inhaler technique is appalling. No medication was getting into her lungs! And, she uses it throughout the ENTIRE movie. I thought I had ruined the movie for him and apologized when it was over. He didn't seem to think it was a big deal.

Next up was *The Buena Vista Social Club,* and when he was queuing it up, he said he had enjoyed all the comments last time. He had never watched a movie with someone who commented the whole time. "I mean, it wasn't *Mystery Science Theater 3000* or anything," he said. I smiled at this non-compliment, relieved that he felt this way. Then I promptly let him down, falling asleep to the beautiful music, sans commentary. Another fail at initiating intimacy through movie watching! The next day I purchased the *Buena Vista Social Club* soundtrack. I still have that CD.

I would wait until he fell asleep and then sneak out to the semi-dark living room to read my non-pharmacy school textbooks. The first time he caught me, he very sweetly asked if I was having trouble sleeping. I should have said, yes, instead of honestly telling him that spending time with him was cutting into my precious reading time. He slowly repeated that truth I had just spoken aloud and looked offended. I should have told him that this was a habit of mine and that books are always better when you read them when you are not supposed to. Instead, I gave up explaining myself and just went to bed.

Once, during exam week while I was held up studying non-stop at my parents' house, Mister Ghost sent me flowers. My mom brought them to me and I asked her who they were from—genuinely perplexed. It didn't seem like something Mister Ghost would do. Flowers were not practical and they were expensive. She just laughed and said, "Oh, I don't know, maybe your boyfriend?"

It still hadn't seemed real to me that I had a boyfriend. I had never gotten flowers before. The card said, "I love you." Mister Ghost had made a big deal out of telling me he thought he was falling in love with me, but I don't remember exactly when he said it. Later in life, when I thought I was completely unlovable, I would refer to the card, proof that at one point someone loved me. I had it in writing. Yes, of course, I still have the card.

As Mister Ghost and I spent more and more time together, my scheming roommate was hard at work sabotaging my entire life. One morning, I opened my eyes to her doing arm curls with her free-weights directly over my head. She was smiling down at me. I soon realized she had turned off my alarm clock, and not for the first time. I couldn't believe it. I had been late every morning for days and couldn't understand why my alarm wasn't going off. Psycho.

She also put Gain laundry detergent in my electric tea kettle, ruining my sacred morning coffee routine. I turned it on and thought I had gotten a faint whiff of the distinctive Gain smell. I didn't think anything of it at first. Then the kettle boiled over with bubbles and all I could smell was Gain. What a strange choice. If, by some miracle, I hadn't smelled the Gain, what was swallowing a bunch of Gain really going to do to me? I had to remind myself this was the same woman who thought she couldn't get pregnant if she had sex in a pool. I also had to remind myself that when Winona Ryder gave Heather a cleaning fluid cocktail in the movie *Heathers*, Heather choked, went smashing through a glass table, and died.

So, I threw away the tea kettle and started sleeping at my parents' house. I only went back to the room when I knew she would not be there. Mister Ghost and I had an elaborate system where he would call a friend in our dorm to knock on the door and see if she was there and then we would head over to pick up a few items and get out as quickly as possible.

The last time I saw her, I passed her on Franklin Street and without even stopping, she informed me over her shoulder that she had put all my food from the refrigerator onto my desk. I couldn't believe she didn't even stop walking. I was with a bunch of people from pharmacy school and all of our mouths dropped. There is no telling how long she lived with that food out on my desk. For all I know she soaked it in Gain to avoid spoilage. She was the owner of the dorm refrigerator, so she was within her rights, but I didn't get why she was so mad.

I know what you're thinking, Girl Code. But what you don't know is that earlier that year she met my friend Brett, who I was just friends with, and convinced herself that he was the perfect man for her. Holly had asked me if I had a friend with a truck and that was Brett. She rode with him to pick up some wood and at the end of that ride she told me she had met *the one*. It was fine by me, but he wasn't interested. She said she just wanted to be friends with Mister Ghost too, so I thought we could all be friends together. Apparently not.

When I discovered my roommate was a saboteur and maybe an incompetent murderess, I wasn't sure where to live next. Two pharmacy school classmates (who had laughed at me the night of the fire alarm) approached me on the bus and invited me to live with them in an apartment off campus. I told them I would have to think about it.

After going through my options—psycho dorm mate or my parents' house—two classmates as roommates seemed like the only way to go. Mister Ghost had said I could live with him and his best friend, but that seemed … premature.

When I told my father the plan, he asked, "Do you even know their last names?" I didn't.

My new apartment was in the same complex as one of Mister Ghost's best friends. He lived in the building next to ours, with his girlfriend. It seemed like kismet but ended up being a curse. Mister Ghost broke up with me soon after we moved into those apartments, citing "different energy levels". Seriously, he told me he had too much energy and I didn't have enough. No one had ever commented on my energy level before, including him. I thought it was a nice way for him to say that I had never slept with him. I didn't want to talk more about that, so I didn't ask too many questions about how exactly he was measuring our energy levels. Was he taking blood samples while I was sleeping?

I had never kissed anyone when I met Mister Ghost. So of course, I was nervous and didn't know what I was doing. I avoided physical intimacy to the point where he asked me if I had been abused. I really went out of my way not to kiss him. Anxiety would take over and it didn't even matter if I wanted to, I just couldn't do it.

Eventually, it happened. While we were sitting side by side at my computer in my dorm room. My roommate had just left the room to go to the bathroom and he grabbed me. I was too stunned to kiss back. My first experience of the sneak attack kiss. I shared this story with my new roommates who didn't laugh at me, but rather sat me down and told me to close my eyes and imagine myself kissing someone I wanted to kiss. Instead, I quickly shut then opened my eyes to see the both of them with their eyes closed and smiles on their faces and I cracked up. It was incredibly sweet of them to try and help me. But I felt I was beyond help.

At the apartment complex, Mister Ghost's friend (we'll call him The Car Guy) paid for an external garage right by where I parked my car—a white, early 90's Acura Legend, a hand-me-down from my parents. I would often see him out there working on his Corvette, but he never spoke, just occasionally waved.

As soon as Mister Ghost broke up with me, he seemed to be around all the time. The day after our breakup, he wrote me a short email inviting me over for dinner. "Why?" I asked him uncomfortably. Maybe he meant to send the email to someone else?

"I have some spaghetti that I was meaning to cook," is what he said. That was it. I passed. I wasn't ready to share comfort food with a man who had just made me feel uncomfortable.

It was all so confusing. At that same time, I was getting emails from Mister Ghost asking where I was going at certain times with specific people. It took me a while to realize that The Car Guy, who was constantly out there "fixing" his car, was reporting my comings and goings to Mister Ghost. Car Guy was a mole!

Once I figured that out, I told my friend Carmen. I pointed him out, and she rolled down the window and yelled the time, her name, and where we were headed. Then we both waved as she sped off. If the mole continued his surveillance after that day, it never got back to me.

Sometimes I would see Mister Ghost's car at our apartment complex on my way back from getting the mail and I would get so nervous my legs would start shaking, to the point that I needed to sit down on the curb. Was he there to see me or his friend? Why was he always around? I would sit on the curb, covered in mail. My roommates would laugh and ask me if I was sure it was his car. His car was covered in very specific bumper stickers. There was no way it wasn't his car! I rolled my eyes as I tried to stand up.

This was the start of our more than 12-year friendship, post-breakup. He would make appearances and disappearances, like a ghost. He was my first Mister, Mister Ghost. He had told me that he was always up late, and I could always text him and he would respond. I tested him on this, and he always passed. I could summon him with a birthday text, and he would appear for days, months, or even years at a time. We would get closer and then he would disappear. When he would appear again, it was as if he had never gone.

Later, when I was living in South Carolina, Mister Ghost decided to go back to school to study astrophysics. I was comfortably playing house with my sister Katie and working as a retail pharmacist. We had been emailing and he told me that for his spring break he would come visit for a week. I took a week off from work and when the time came, he became a ghost and I got this email at the last hour.

Friday, March 9, 2007 12:02 AM:

"Mary,

Sorry this is coming so late, but I won't be able to come down for spring break next week. My financial aid refund didn't come through until last week, and I've been busy with studying for a couple of midterms tomorrow, so I haven't had a chance to do anything. Sorry I can't make it down. And sorry for not calling back yet. I didn't check my voicemail until last night after I realized you'd sent me a text message. I've got to get back to studying, but I'll write more later."

I got my fifth tattoo that week, "Hope Dies Last." It is a phrase that I first heard uttered by Joey Potter on *Dawson's Creek*. I had taken it to heart. My email response to him was lengthy, so I will just share three sentences. (The following is the exact text from the email. I had deemed the message important enough that I printed it out and stapled it into my journal).

"As a result of your most recent brush off, I know my next tattoo **Hope Dies Last**. I know you said you were sorry in the email but in my attempts to become more assertive I needed to let you know how I feel. I feel like I was an afterthought and fuck you, I am not an afterthought." It was a while before we chatted again.

After Mister Ghost had originally told me he loved me, he started asking me about marriage on a regular basis. It wasn't with a ring or any formal proposal, but just the inquiry.

Could I have married him?

At first, I thought it was just another one of his tests. I wasn't sure what the right answer was, so I answered truthfully and said, no. He kept asking. I kept feeling bad for saying no. We were so young.

The more I learned about the dysfunction and abuse in his family, the more I understood him and why he was asking. Mister Ghost desperately wanted his own family. He is who he is because of the mental and physical abuse he endured at the hands of his stepfather, who he only ever referred to as "the fat man". I never met the fat man. I just saw his pants.

I had asked to powder my nose while at his parents' house one afternoon. Mister Ghost escorted me to the bathroom just to make sure everything looked "normal": toilet flushed and no embarrassing reading material lying around. Before he left me to it, he held up a pair of the fat man's pants that were slung over the towel rack. To this day, I have never seen a pair of pants that big.

Growing up, the fat man repeatedly told Mister Ghost that he was worthless. So, Mister Ghost always made sure he made more money than his stepdad; there was a specific percentage more he always had to make. Between all that pressure and his lack of what my friend Sarah calls "home training" (aka manners), most people thought he was just a jerk, including my family and most of my friends.

Much like me, Mister Ghost was not good at small talk. I brought him to a family gathering for my youngest sister Megan's dance recital. My parents had family visiting from out of state, and my Uncle Ray asked Mister Ghost where he was from and he responded, Mississippi. Uncle Ray asked, "Have you ever been to the North?" Mister Ghost replied, "No. I have not."

Uncle Ray's only response to this was, "You should come to the North because people wear sweaters inside." Then Uncle Ray walked away. Mister Ghost went on to have similar interactions with my other family members.

Within 15 minutes of meeting my sister Katie, Mister Ghost called her a bitch—to my face, not hers. If he had made the mistake of saying it to her face, she probably would have cursed him out and then left, taking me with her, so that she could tell me all the reasons I should never see him again, concluding her speech by reminding me that she is always right. It's annoying because she has reminded me of this often throughout our lives. And she was, in fact, always right.

When he met my boss and coworkers from Eckerd Pharmacy, they told me it was never going to last because he didn't drink coffee and there was also something about him that made them think he would kill me.

That night, I fell asleep in his dorm room and didn't call my parents. This was during the summer, so I was living back at home. My mother called the pharmacy and my coworkers told my mom that Mister Ghost must have killed me. That was the first and only option they thought of. I came home to my mother hysterically crying. After a brief hug, she screamed at me for a while. I walked into work and the screaming continued. "Mary! We just knew he had killed you!" No one liked him, not even a little bit.

I also got a parking ticket as a result of falling asleep at his dorm. I could've just paid the fine, but I wanted to dispute the ticket. I wasn't comfortable calling Mister Ghost my boyfriend because he was so inconsistent, so I never did. This bothered him, a lot. To dispute the ticket, I had to fill out some paperwork and describe the situation, and so he asked how I was going to refer to him. He thought I was caught and I would have to say "my boyfriend," but I wrote, "a resident of Mangum dorm," and showed it to him. He laughed and shook his head.

It was during this summer that I had to go to Greensboro for a month to work for CVS, for free. It was part of my pharmacy school curriculum. The moment I walked into the CVS, the pharmacist introduced himself and said he was filling a prescription for his wife who had a "raging UTI" and then he had to leave and would see me tomorrow. While he was filling the prescription, he was chit-chatting with me and asked me if I had a boyfriend. I said I did, with a smile. He scowled, "Break up with him! You are too young to be in a relationship. You need to date the fat ones and the skinny ones and the tall ones." I did not respond. I stood frozen, with my cross-body bag slung around me. He said it one more time, "I am serious, break up with him," and then he left. Even complete strangers did not support my relationship.

Once Mister Ghost got his first real job, he bought his own yellow Corvette with a vanity plate that in Linux code meant "mount me," as in mounting a hard drive. When I asked him why he got that car, he said, "The chicks love it," and I had to inform him that the ladies that love a flashy Corvette are not the type of ladies he needed in his life. I'd like to think he took my words to heart, but he had at least one accident I was aware of and got some speeding tickets, so the Corvette didn't last too long in any case.

We shared a similar taste in music and had several conversations about Cake songs. He once found an old iPod while he was living in New York City, and extracted all the music from it, burned the MP3s onto CDs, and sent them to me wrapped up in old cereal boxes for protection. At the time he told me it was his music and I was so happy to get such a huge quantity of music that when it arrived, I immediately picked a CD at random and put it in the computer. It was a live version of the song "Edit the Sad Parts" by Modest Mouse. It brought me to tears. The song is beautiful and heartbreaking, but right then it felt like it was the perfect description of how I was choosing to edit out the sad parts of our relationship. I felt like the sad parts were only my sad parts, so I was willing to pretend we had no sad parts.

Mister Ghost had originally moved to New York to pursue a PhD, a reaction to the girl he was seeing getting serious and her wanting them to get a dog. Appropriate. He had apparently given up on the whole marriage thing. She followed him. He described her only as the nurse. I was curious about her, but he didn't tell me much. I asked him what perfume she wore. I thought this would tell me everything I needed to know about her. He said she wore Curve, and "it permeated everything she wore". I bought a bottle the next day at Eckerd. It was a bargain at less than 20 dollars and after I sprayed it on my wrist, I felt like I had just coated myself in pepper.

How are they both not sneezing all the time? I ended up giving it away to one of Katie's friends, saying it was a gift and just not for me.

He and Curve girl eventually broke up, but they couldn't afford to live separately in New York, so they were still living together. He revealed that to me after a lovely afternoon hanging out in Chapel Hill, full of nostalgia. He said he wanted to get his roommate a UNC t-shirt. We were walking around and talking, and he had been playing the pronoun game when referring to his roommate, but when it came time to find the t-shirt, the sales lady persisted and got it out of him: female, size extra small. The sales lady quickly removed herself from the conversation and fled back to the register as he loudly explained that yes, his roommate is not only an extra small female, but the nurse and former New York girlfriend. It was the extra small part that stung the most. There is nothing about me that is extra small. We didn't speak for a while after that.

Several months go by and we are back in touch, exchanging emails.

Mary,

"I am a very bad friend. Yes, I am. Just say it. I can't even use school as an excuse, but I probably will anyway. Spring break wasn't as relaxing as I thought it would be. I also found a few more gray hairs. I burned a new DVD for you since I've added a few more things and I wasn't sure what your stance on Wu-Tang and Britney Spears is. That, I promise, will be out in the mail in the next couple of weeks."

He thinks we are friends? We were not friends. There is not a name for what we are. I also started to question how well he really knew me. When I told him I got my first tattoo, he asked if it was a butterfly. A freaking butterfly?! Now he has to ask what my "stance" on Wu-Tang and Britney Spears is?! I am not sure if I have ever been more offended by a question. Instead of dedicating paragraphs of my email back to him with an ode to the one and only Britney Jean Spears, I tell him I have moved back to North Carolina. He says he will be in town for a wedding, so he asks me to dinner. A nice gesture, but I developed a migraine the morning of our date. As dinner time closed in, I became nauseated. What did I think was about to happen? Why was I putting myself through this again?

He didn't have a car, so I had to pick him up (and drop him off) from The Car Guy's house, aka the mole. While he was in the bathroom during our dinner, our waitress asked me if we were on a first date, which stunned me. By then we had been on countless "dates." After a long silence which included me looking directly into her eyes trying to find the right words, she finally said, "Well, it looks like it is going well!" Then she winked and walked away.

I had on a black dress with leggings and cowboy boots. Right before I left, I lifted up the back of my dress in the doorway and showed him the tattoo that he inspired, "Hope Dies Last." He touched my arm and my heart fell to my toes. He had this weird look in his eye, like he was about to be vulnerable. But my emotions were maxed out; I bolted out the door.

He asked me to a cookout the next day, with all his closest friends. These people were his family and I had met all of them before, but they didn't seem to remember me. They were probably wondering why I was there.

I did meet one girl at the beginning of the evening who I had never met before. His friends were all taking turns talking to me, but as usual he avoided being in the same room as me. When I finally went looking for him, he was in a room playing a Nintendo Wii game with the new girl I had been introduced to but didn't know, and I heard her say, "We could never play this in our apartment, it's too small." It hit me like a ton of bricks. They had all spent the day together, that was the nurse and they still lived together, she was part of his family. I was not.

Why was I there? I could not get out of there fast enough.

He seemed puzzled about why I was leaving so abruptly. As I was taking way too long to get my shoes on because my hands were shaking, he asked me to email him more often. He said he was bad about it too, but "just e-mail me more." Why did he pick now to plead with me? It was just the two of us at the door and I was about to burst into tears at any second. I could not look up or say goodbye.

I cried all the way home, stopping off to see my friend Monte who was living with her twin sister and her husband. I needed a Monte hug, the only hug I ever welcomed. I can still remember my first Monte hug. It was after our fall break in pharmacy school and the first time we had been apart since we had met and she just came up to me in the hallway and gave me what felt like a full body love squeeze. It felt so genuine. It made every other hug I had ever received feel like a lie. I thought maybe it was a one-time deal, but it turns out I get this same magic hug every single time, even 20 years later. Anyway, Monte's sister's husband looked at me as I walked into their kitchen and asked me how I was. I couldn't answer him because I was crying so hard. With all three of them looking at me, he filled the awkward silence and said well, it looked like I was doing really well, and we all laughed. He snapped me out of it. I had been forever hopeful that I would break through and be the one that Mister Ghost would always want to be in a room with. I was not her. I was never her. I needed to get that through my head. Why could I not smell more like pepper? It was not meant to be. Why was I still forcing it after all these years?

Crafty has a "volver" tattoo. In Spanish it means "to return." I was with her when she got it and I know the person she kept returning to, but I didn't understand the power of the word at the time.

Somehow, she kept falling asleep during the session. She said it was the sound of the needle that was lulling her to sleep. I was there to get a tattoo of a giant ship emerging from dark clouds to mark a new beginning. The tattoo artist was so excited for us, he yelled, "To new beginnings!" as we walked out the door.

Eventually, Crafty was able to break free of *the volver*, but that is not my story to tell. I have my own version of the volver tattoo and it is just a red circle. Mister Ghost and I had only seemed capable of going round and round. It was a vicious cycle that I kept returning to. I only had room for one vicious cycle in my life and that was the one I had already been in for years: coffee in the a.m. and alcohol in the p.m. Maybe you're familiar with it.

After I got my Monte hug, all four of us were standing around the kitchen sink, and I refocused on what was important. I needed to be around people who calmed me and made me laugh. Mister Ghost and I did not communicate at all for several years after this kitchen-sink realization.

Several years later, I found out he never finished getting his PhD in astrophysics, there was something about a disagreement with his advisor, so he dropped out and was back living in North Carolina. I summoned him with another birthday text and just like that he was back in my life. He told me that he had been writing his dissertation about Pluto's moons. I had to read that again. Pluto's moons? I didn't even know Pluto had one moon, let alone moons. Why in the world did we care about Pluto's moons so much? Especially since everyone knows Pluto lost its planet status. I told him I didn't want to spread gossip, but I heard it was because Pluto couldn't keep its orbit tidy.

So, as per usual, we started catching up without addressing anything that happened in the past. It was just a brunch. I wanted nothing special from him anymore. We can just meet up and do what friends do.

He said he was going to help me write this book, the one you are reading, about my online dating experiences. I got excited to work on the project with him. He was teaching at a college near his hometown in Thomasville, so we planned our next dinner for the night he would finish with exams.

He came to Durham and we had a relaxed dinner at a restaurant I had been to several times before. I arrived first, as usual, so I was sitting when he walked in. I had ordered a martini before he got there and as I took a sip; I realized my legs were not shaking and I was totally calm. Perhaps it was possible for us to finally transition into a normal friendship?

I am not sure why, but I was so confident in our newly established friendship that after dinner I invited him to Carrboro to see my place and to meet my cocker spaniels, Sophie and Lucy. When we got to the house, I turned on my satellite radio and it was playing the band Grizzly Bear. Mister Ghost became animated and said he had just been listening to them in his car. We still had the same taste in music. I offered him a drink and went over all my beverage options, because I remembered he was a beer drinker and I don't keep beer in my house. He chose what I remember him drinking in college, rum and Coke. My Captain Morgan's bottle had dust on it. I quickly wiped it off with my sleeve as I passed it to him. Was it from when I wanted to try making hot buttered rum? It sounded so festive! And I always keep cans of Coke around because it's the only thing that cures my hangovers.

I made myself a grapefruit Perrier with Pinnacle vodka. I used to buy Pinnacle because it came in a larger plastic bottle and not only was it cost effective but it wasn't horrible. We were drinking and talking, and he decided to read my first online dating story, about Mister Portugal, out loud. He had a red pen in hand and he made corrections as he read, pacing around my living room. It was surreal to hear my dating story coming out of his mouth.

When he finished, he paused and looked at me and asked if that had all really happened to me. I told him, *you know it did, all of it.* He looked at me for a while and asked if I had more stories like this. I said yes, several. He shook his head.

He asked if he could stay over because it was late and he had been drinking. I invited him to stay in my guest room. He repeated the words "guest room" while looking in my eyes.

We continued talking and I was working my way through all the books on my giant living room bookshelves. I was literally holding my favorite book, *Magical Thinking* by Augusten Burroughs, and very enthusiastically telling him all about it, when he ripped it from my hand and threw it across the room, and then he grabbed me and started kissing me. He got me again with the sneak attack kiss!

It didn't feel real, I felt like I was in a movie. I went with it. I was finally at his energy level and it only took two martinis and several Perrier and vodkas. It was the first and only time we slept together. Luckily, I had brunch plans at 10 am the next morning with Super Dirty Hutch (SDH), so after I walked the dogs, alone, as I did every morning, I was the one to wake him up and kick him out. We didn't talk about it, just one final kiss and he left. I did offer him a Coke in case he was hung over. He just looked at me and said "no more Coke!"

I arrived at brunch in the same dress as the night before and with my hair not as perfectly pinned back and there was this one piece that would not stay pinned no matter what I did. I was still trying to tame it as I walked into the restaurant. It gave me away. SDH took one look at me, smiled, and asked what had happened last night.

I had no idea what sleeping with him meant, and I guess it just meant goodbye. I have not seen or heard from him since. I stopped texting and emailing. I had found my way out. It was finally time for me to give up the ghost.

Four

Mister First Online Date

Charleston, SC circa 2007

My first online date was courtesy of eHarm. Remember those commercials with the old white man telling you, with a smile, that he had a "scientific system" for dating? All the while, Natalie Cole was singing "This Will Be (An Everlasting Love)" in the background. He had a trilogy of power names and looked like Mister Rogers' evil twin. He was letting the world know that he had the key to finding the love of all our lives. All you had to do was sign up and pay—a lot.

In 2007, eHarm cost more than the other online dating sites. When the wrinkly, wealthy proprietor (and self-appointed spokesman) looked through the screen and told me that he'd figured out the 29 dimensions of compatibility, I just knew I'd be in good hands. I was going to trust his process, for sure. As my coworker Mike says, "You pays your money and you takes your chances."

If you are not familiar with eHarm, the way it used to work was that if you managed to catch the attention of what seemed like an endless sea of generic white men, then you were sent five questions from the eHarm questionnaire. Then you had to choose your answer from the multiple choices provided by eHarm. The one question that every single man sent me: "If you were taken by your date to a party where you knew no one, how would you respond?"

I don't remember all the provided answers, but it was something like, *(a) stick close to your date and wait to be introduced, (b) branch out on your own, and (c) some scenario where you were capable of doing both*. I knew the intent of the question was to gauge my level of independence, but I was never sure what the correct answer was. What were my potential suitors looking for? Instead of answering truthfully, I picked the middle of the road answer, (c).

The question I always sent: "How often do you find yourself laughing?" Most people responded with the middle of the road answer as well. Maybe we were all playing the same game—when in doubt pick (c). Anyway, if you answered his questions, then you had the privilege of being able to send him five of the form questions. If answered, then, and only then, you finally got to the part where you could ask whatever you wanted. Most people asked more questions from the pre-formulated eHarm bank of available questions. It was mind numbing.

It wasn't long before I was spending every night answering the same questions, just so that I could move onto the "next step" again. Every man started to seem like the same faceless contender—exactly the same. And most men of a certain age, at least in South Carolina at that time, were looking for the same type of woman. These women were fit, bubbly, and covered in Lilly Pulitzer or a similar floral assault. They were "wife material". Personally, I did not know any woman who fit this description but I was exposed to them during my various woman-about-town activities: when they came into my pharmacy or joined my classes at the Pilates studio or when we ended up side by side at the nail salon. I overheard their conversations and scrutinized their fashion sense. It was a little glimpse into their world.

I often sat silently outraged, my inner monologue sounding something like, "She paid three HUNDRED dollars for a pillow? She played tennis for an hour and walked a few miles BEFORE coming to this Pilates class? Oh, she doesn't work? At all? Could redecorating your home really take up ALL of your time?" It all made me cringe. I could not relate. These women seemed to be in constant fear. If they didn't work out constantly, keep the house perfect, and only spend time with their kids and husband, then their lives might all fall apart and their husbands would leave them.

Right before I started high school, I was babysitting my cousins who lived in an affluent village in Westchester County, New York. I was at their yacht club one day when I overheard some of the women conversing about their favorite subject: husbands. The wives just didn't seem happy. This is when my ideas on marriage started to change. These yacht clubbers seemed to have it all, but when I got close enough to examine their lives, I didn't want anything they had. Once I realized marriage was not an inevitable part of life and would definitely not be a part of mine (thanks ladies!), I never looked back. Ever since, no one has been able to sell me on making the choice to marry.

Maybe my non-wife energy was why I wasn't having much luck securing a date by the end of the e-questioning. If the eHarm men didn't like the way I answered any of the five questions, then that was it. I was dead in the water. Apparently, a wife-type would not even think to branch out on their own at a party and should stay firmly at the side of their husband.

You might be asking yourself, "Why did she subject herself to this eHarm?" I was asking myself that every day. But I knew I just had to find the one guy that wasn't like everyone else; a guy who didn't want a woman who looked like everyone else. Maybe he too had a crazy work schedule that prohibited him from having an active social life, so he was online dating like me, muddling through and believing in the old man's scientific approach?

If I made it to the later stages of the questioning, I would describe myself as having reddish hair that I dyed myself, and tattoos. That did not scream wife-y to most of these faceless men. When I would reveal that I was a pharmacist, most of the time that sealed my fate. Since I never had the pleasure of speaking to them in person, I don't know exactly why this was such a turn off.

My sister Katie (now a chef and married business owner with a kid), whom I lived with in Charleston, was always trying to set me up. Enter Chance, who I actually met face to face. How can you say no to taking a Chance on love? So, Chance and I had one dinner date that Katie and her friend also attended, but they sat somewhere else in the restaurant. It was that kinda date.

Chance started the date by lying to me. He asked if I had ever been to the restaurant we had just sat down in, and I said I had never been. When I asked him the same question, he said he had the same answer as me, nope never been. But as the words left his mouth, the bartender came over and put a beer in front of him and greeted him by name. We both laughed.

Chance is a mechanic and really enjoys his work. He makes a pretty good living. I tell him what I do, and, suddenly, he stops eating and says, "I never even went to college." I knew it was over after that, even though I don't care if a prospective partner or anyone has gone to stinking college. I could tell he had decided I was definitely not the girl for him. Chance barely smiled or made eye contact after that.

The sole reason Mister First Online Date Man caught my attention, from the 87 other guys I was answering to, was because he asked me three extremely specific questions. Granted, they were wife-interview questions, like all the rest, but these had me instantly intrigued. They were promising, or at least alluding to, a certain kind of life. Even though I knew I would answer them "WRONG," I decided to be honest.

I had at least three alarm clocks set to go off at different times, including a CD-player alarm clock that plays The Hives at maximum volume. It's set for at least a half hour before I need to get up, so that I can snooze it a few times.

If you are not familiar with The Hives, they are an upbeat, fast-paced, well-dressed Swedish rock band. Their 2004 album, Tyrannosaurus Hives, was the only CD that was ever in my CD player alarm clock. It did the trick. To start your day with your heart pumping out of your chest, just set the volume to 50 and enjoy track one, "Abra Cadaver." I recommend experiencing it yourself, focusing on the lyrics. I didn't ever need another song because this one was doing double duty. In addition to startling me awake, it was also my daily reminder not to become dead inside.

I read a magazine article that said if you have a hard time getting up and you hit snooze more than once, then you should place your alarm across the room because it will force you to get up and blindly stumble to it. The flailing in the dark part is what might help the waking process. So, I had another alarm at the other end of my bedroom. The third was the backup alarm that was shoved in the top drawer of my nightstand. If all else failed, I would eventually hear a muffled beeping noise that would annoy me enough to wake me up. Mister Loner, who I met later, as will you, declared that if I had a band, it would be called "Mary and the Alarms".

First question: Can you live your life without an alarm clock?

Answer: No.

Second question: Would you give up your job to work for my business, helping sell mustard and ketchup to local restaurants?

As you know, I am a pharmacist. I have spent hard-earned money and worked like a dog to get through pharmacy school. And no, I would not be quitting my job to undersell French's and Heinz.

Answer: No.

Third question: Would you participate in my family's yearly vacation to Africa to hunt big game?

I would love to go to Africa on safari but count me out for hunting or going with family. If it came to it, I would rather be out there pretending to kill animals than share a meal with a family that is not my own, especially a family that thinks it is not only ok but fun to kill animals.

Answer: No.

These questions reminded me of an interview Oprah did with Lance Armstrong's ex-wife Kristen. Kristen said that she should have known it wasn't going to work out when Lance asked her in the very beginning to give up her job, car, home, and dog to support his life. I am sorry she thought that living his life would be better than living her own, but, because of her (and Oprah!), I wouldn't make that mistake. Thank you, Kristen! She now appears to be thriving, having written several books as well as running marathons and writing for *Runner's World*. Perhaps it sounds weird to say you are proud of someone you never met, but I am. Also, what kind of monster asks someone to give up their dog for them? Come on.

One of the first things I made sure to mention when I first met Mister First Online Date was that I had two cocker spaniels, who I loved very much and couldn't imagine my life without. So, in addition to everything else I am not doing (like getting married), I will not be giving them up either. Don't even ask.

I still have no idea why we agreed to meet after the final round of questioning. He was not what I was looking for, and I thought, for sure, I was not what he was looking for. Nevertheless, when he wanted to meet for lunch (he made it all very last minute and dramatic), for curiosity's sake—and hunger's—I went. It turned out we only lived five minutes from each other. I thought maybe this was a sign that it was going to be easy and meant to be. He was about to leave town because two family members were very sick, but before he hit the road, he could meet me at this barbeque place that I had never heard of.

If you have ever been to Charleston, you know that it is virtually impossible to get a bad meal, and living there with my sister, who is a chef, meant that our lives were food-centric. I didn't have to travel far for good grub. But it sounded like it had to be a quick lunch, and I was trying out a new restaurant in the process. To me, it seemed painless, and my friend Peter has always said, "When it is right, it is easy." Thank you, Peter. After I agreed to the place and meeting time, I began to panic about what to wear. I had never been on a lunch date before. Luckily, I had a "going out" uniform, so I just threw it on, spraying myself down with Thierry Mugler's Angel perfume, since there was no time for a shower. If you are familiar with this scent, you can probably smell me right now. It is strong and better suited for nighttime; not mixed with daytime and Southern barbeque.

I had purchased identical tube-top shirt-dresses in every available color that TJ Maxx stocked in my size. They were actually too short to be a dress and longer than your average shirt, so I just paired one with jeans. Dresses with jeans were a popular look in the early aughts, according to me and Jessica Alba (net worth = $200 million). I would just alternate these shirt-dresses with jeans and thoroughly worn black or brown Rainbow brand flip-flops. The element that made this ensemble my "going out" uniform was giant, beaded, peacock feather earrings (I had picked them up while on vacation in Maine with my family when I was ten years old).

When I had just started my first job as a retail pharmacist at Eckerd, I had the pleasure of working with Sarah, an intern from The Medical University of South Carolina who took the time to share with me that my makeup could be doing more... for me. Sarah had been a makeup artist. I was already in awe of her intelligence and grace under pressure and now this. She was almost too good to be true! Sarah bought me my first Lancôme Juicy Tube (which I promptly lost) as a birthday present and started me down the path to high-priced face paint, and after I saw what it could do for me, I was hooked. Between the acne I could not shake and a generalized, pervasive insecurity about my appearance, I needed all the help I could get. I started to enjoy the ritual of putting on makeup.

This new obsession resulted in me visiting a MAC store every time I was on vacation in a major city. I always wanted to know what else I should be using and how to use it. I will never forget being in a MAC store near Oakland, California. The MAC lady looked at me with pity in her eyes as she figured out what I already knew. Looking up from her computer she said, "Honey, there is not a MAC store around you. I'm not sure what you're going to do." I told her that's why I'm testing out products now and learning how to use them, then I can just buy more of what I like online. She shook her head and muttered, "I guess." I got so into it that one of my other interns, Kristen, asked me to do her makeup on her wedding day. This I did not feel qualified for. At all. After I reluctantly agreed to do it, I went to Barnes and Noble and bought a couple of big picture books on how to apply makeup. I studied every night before I went to sleep. That was the first and last time I ever did someone else's makeup. I could not handle the stress and was so focused on all things makeup that on my way out the door, without looking, I grabbed a vintage white lace shawl to put over my strapless dress.

I was in charge of reading a bible passage during this Catholic church wedding. I had way too much exposed skin to be up on an altar but because of all my makeup cramming, I didn't notice that one of my cocker spaniels had peed on the shawl. There was a noticeably large yellow stain on it and, as I noticed after wrapping it around my shoulders in church, the shawl smelled. I mean, it reeked!

"What's that smell?" my sister Katie kept asking as we settled uncomfortably into a pew. As usual, I had on way too much perfume, Romance by Ralph Lauren, so I could not smell it at first. Katie sniffed me and realized what had happened. Sigh. Our faces were scrunched in disgust when I heard my name called out from the altar. It was time for my dog-piss-stained self to make her way up. I quickly read the Word of the Lord and then speed walked back to my seat, hoping the pee smell wasn't wafting into the pews as I passed them.

On our way home from the wedding, Katie and I bought a bunch of gas-station candy to celebrate my successful bridal make up and Katie's wedding cake. She had been in charge of the cake and cupcakes. The man at the gas station laughed at the amount of candy we were buying while still in our wedding gear. "I guess you fit into your dresses, now you can eat your candy!" he chimed in.

My fashion philosophy has pretty much stayed the same since I was a teen. My clothes are mostly plain but my accessories, bags, and shoes are what people notice and comment on. Once, there was a MAC-store employee who watched me come to her counter and the first thing she said to me was, "You are a lot to take in." This came from the mouth of a lady who had a shaved head covered in tattoos and a face covered in layers of bright and beautiful high-priced face paint. What a compliment!

Anyway, back at the barbecue restaurant with Mister First Online Date, I could feel him taking me in as we were standing there waiting to order. When I looked up, he smiled and touched my earrings and said, "You dressed up." We sat and talked. I saw that he had some of my good friend Peter's features. He looked familiar so that set me at ease, perhaps maybe too at ease.

Mister First Online Date mentioned that he's an inventor as well as a condiments guy. He was working on a portable surfboard. I know, you're thinking: "Wait, aren't they already portable?" I brought that to his attention. Quickly, without smiling, he said, no. He was working on one you could fold up and put in your suitcase. That type of portable. But he hadn't worked out the folding part just yet.

Turns out, he was also a Clemson cheerleader! Then he showed me his one and only tattoo: a Clemson paw print on his leg. He proudly shared that all the members of his squad have the same tattoo. "So, there are several people who chose to have this same paw print tattoo?" I asked, thinking this might be worse than a tribal tattoo situation. I couldn't hide it; the disgust was written all over my face. I know, I don't know when I became a tattoo snob.

When I told him I had tattoos, including one on the middle of my back of the chemical structure for caffeine, I don't think he believed me. I know he didn't. When we stood up after the 'cue, he went behind me and lifted my shirt without asking and gaped at the mosaic on my back while we were standing in the middle of the restaurant. Damn that tube-top shirtdress!

Not cool. He not only lifted up my shirt to take a peek without asking, he did it in front of a dining room of strangers. I like to control who sees which tattoos, and there he was just helping himself and showing others without permission. Well, with that flick of the wrist there went what little trust I had in this man.

Another tattoo on my back, directly next to the caffeine structure, is "Run Devil, Run" written in cursive. It was the name of a song by Jenny Lewis and The Watson Twins that I was obsessed with. It's a beautiful song. The only two words in the entire song are "run" and "devil" until the last two words, "from love". I thought it would help keep "the devil" out of my love life. Turns out, it takes much more than a tattoo, or maybe it's that the devil is just not a fan of the folksier stylings of the aughts' queen of indie pop?

Then he noticed the tattoos on my toes. I have the pi symbol on one big toe and a cross on the other big toe. The pi was my first tattoo, a result of the Darren Aronofsky movie of the same name. I was forced to see the movie after a man I didn't know grabbed my arm as I was reading the back of the DVD container at VisArt, a movie rental place. The stranger told me I had to watch it and that it would change my life. But he had scared me and while he held my arm, he stared into my eyes so intently that I became panicked about what would happen if I didn't rent it.

As it turns out, he was right, it did change my life. I decided to get the pi symbol to remind me that there is a mathematical order to the universe. The cross is to remind me that there is something creating that mathematical order. Science and religion were very much at odds for me when I was working in a retail pharmacy in The South. The toe ink helped me find balance, or at least attempt to. I found myself having conversations with the elderly about why they should be paying, in some cases, hundreds of dollars for their cholesterol-lowering medications when God was going to take them when it was their time anyway. Fair question.

Looking at the chemical structure of the caffeine tattoo prompted my date to ask if I wanted a coffee. Suddenly, magically, he had some extra time and could hit the road after that. So, against my better judgment, I got into his jeep, which had a shocking number of library books in the back seat. They were all thick, hardcover books just thrown back there, taking up both seats. It seemed both careless and ambitious at the same time. When I would go to the library, I left with two books, three max. If I have more than that, it's overwhelming. There must have been 30 or so books back there. I had so many questions and no time to look at them to see what he was reading about. Why was he taking a road trip with just books in his back seat? Maybe they were all about surfboard design? I would never know. (I don't offer many dating tips but, yes, before getting into a stranger's car on a first date, check the back seat. I always do. Safety first!)

Mister First Online Date referred to us as "we" when speaking with the barista. "We live right down the road," as if we were suddenly a couple. We sat down and talked about plans, mostly his plans. I don't remember much of what he said because the coffee shop started to play *Naked Eye* by Luscious Jackson, which was one of the songs I was reintroduced to when Mister Ghost mailed me a bunch of mp3s he burned onto CDs and stuffed into old cereal boxes so they were "protected". I was in my head, wondering why Mister Ghost took the time to send me all that music, and was also trying to picture him listening to Luscious Jackson. Whose music did he send to me?

We had just one cup of coffee, as he talked at me, and then it was officially time for him to get on the road. When he dropped me back at my car, he attempted what became a brief kiss on the cheek. I was not expecting or desiring a kiss. I instinctively turned my head and his lips landed on the side of my face. Yes, it was the dreaded sneak-attack kiss. I hate the sneak-attack kiss. It was too soon, of course, and this one felt more like a goodbye kiss from someone you have known a while and kissed a million times, not someone you just met. He was trying to skip a few steps and instantly put us in a relationship. I just wasn't ready to sell condiments without all my alarms.

Five

Mister Confused Turtle Neck

Durham, NC Circa 2008

I had just moved back to North Carolina from South Carolina and started a new job at a CRO in Durham when the IT guy arrived at my desk. He was having a hard time connecting my computer to the right printer, so we started chit chatting and he asked me if I was dating anyone.

CRO stands for Contract Research Organization and the one I work for provides support to the pharmaceutical industry. This takes place in a call center-warehouse with cubicles as far as the eye can see. In response to the amount of people we work with, Mike, an older pharmacist who sat next to me, leaned over one day and said, "Mary, I am better at identifying birds than people around here." Every time someone would say hello to us on their way to the breakroom or the bathroom, he would smile and say, "Hello!" and then when they walked away, he would laugh and ask me, "Who was that?" This happened several times a day.

At work, my every move is timed and watched. I think the management's strategy may be best referred to as "excessive monitoring". The monitoring applies to every aspect of my life: how I smell (more on this in a sec), what I say to the callers, what I eat at work (there are rules against microwaved popcorn and fish), as well as how well I adhere to my scheduled breaks and lunch (I cannot be one second over. NOT ONE!). And, there are no secrets.

One day, I was called into an empty conference room by my supervisor. She said a complaint had been received about the way I smelled. Apparently, my scent was triggering the asthma of one of the people who had an actual office in the building and not a cubicle. I asked for further clarification because every inch of me has a different smell—from my detergent, my shampoo, perfume, lotion … What exactly was I being asked to stop wearing? I could tell that my supervisor did not want to be having this conversation with me. "Can I just ask you to stop wearing all of it?" she said.

At the time, my cubicle was in between the break room and the bathroom. I was also surrounded by hundreds of co-workers, so the various aromas were constant and constantly changing. "Sure," I said, "I'll stop it all." I smiled. "The last thing I want to do is trigger someone's asthma. It certainly would not be a problem to change my detergent and hair care supplies and to switch my lotions to unscented versions and to stop using all my precious perfumes, too."

Ok, I didn't actually say that last bit aloud. I felt terrible. I asked everyone I knew about how I smelled. Had my desire to be heavily perfumed been a burden to my friends? Thankfully, the consensus was no. I needed to ask someone who was always brutally honest with me, with whom I had close contact. I asked my friend and former coworker, Irina, at our weekly martini meeting. After I finished asking her and explaining why I was asking her, she took a sip of her Bikini Martini and, in her delightful Eastern European accent, she said, "Mary, this is bullshit."

The Bikini Martini was not on the drink menu anymore because the restaurant had changed hands. But it was the only thing Irina ever drank there and she was used to ordering it without looking at the menu. Eventually they just gave up trying to explain this and now make it special for her and only her. Once when she was running late, Irina had asked me to order it for her, and I was denied. I needed to have ordered it with an Eastern European accent, I guess. I had never even thought to attempt to duplicate her accent. If you are interested in making a giant Bikini Martini for yourself, it is 4 ounces of coconut rum, 4 ounces of pineapple juice, 2 ounces of vodka, and 1 ounce of grenadine in a martini shaker with ice; shake and serve.

Irina rarely cursed, but she favored the word BULLSHIT. She shook her head, "Don't you dare change a thing!" For several years, Irina and I had worked together in close quarters at a small neighborhood pharmacy, Eckerd. During that time, she often shared her thoughts regarding things in my life that I might've wanted to change: my shoes, eye shadow, purses, diet, etc. She bought me my first-ever purse from Banana Republic and my first big-girl eye shadow palette (from Lancôme, complete with handwritten diagrams of an eye and where to put each color). Not only was she one of my best friends and pharmacy mentors, but she was always elegant, funny, intelligent and stunningly gorgeous.

It shocked me at first, but her bluntness was something I became accustomed to and welcomed. It was on one of our martini nights that a man offered to buy our drinks. I had never had a man I didn't know offer to buy me a drink before or since. The ironic part was that I was drinking coffee on our martini night so that I could stay up and read The Hunger Games Trilogy. My coworker Daphne had loaned the books to me and when she put them on my desk her parting words were, "I am so jealous you get to experience these for the first time." I could not put those books down. They decimated my social life. Mostly. But I could not cancel on Irina.

They made a pot of coffee for me at the bar and I was steadily making my way through it. Irina asked our waitress to point out who exactly offered to buy our drinks and then she proceeded to laugh and declined the offer loudly. "I am married!" Gesturing towards me, she continued, "What will this old man buy you? Your pot of coffee? Why? Better you buy it yourself."

I learned with time that I could trust her completely, from pharmaceutical knowledge to fashion, food, and relationships. I brought her to Sundance with me one year and instead of watching movies all day, she wanted to ski. Skiing was her passion and since she was skiing alone, she would meet different men on the ski lifts and they would ski together for the rest of the day. Irina did not want to waste time going to the bathroom or eating, so she always took to the slopes with one 4-ounce amber bottle from the pharmacy filled with vodka (plus an energy bar).

One day, she skied with a "famous American actor, he was white," Irina told me. That is all she knew about him. It was unclear if he'd told her he was a famous actor or if someone else had to point this out to Irina. It took us several days to put a name to the white American actor.

It was Woody Harrelson. Irina didn't know a lot of famous people, so when we saw celebs in the wild, I would classify them as A-listers, B-listers, C-listers etc., to provide context for her. We mostly saw D-listers like a spikey-headed Ryan Cabrera wearing a white V-neck t-shirt and no coat, standing on a corner in Park City, Utah, surrounded by snow. I get excited to see D-listers, especially one hit wonders from the early aughts who are having trouble letting go of the hair and fashion of their heyday. When I told Irina she had skied with an A-lister, she exclaimed, "I knew it!" I like to imagine her offering Woody a swig of vodka from her amber prescription bottle.

So anyway, I followed Irina's orders, of course, and did not change a thing about my scents. I checked-in with my supervisor a week later to make sure I wasn't triggering anyone's asthma. My supervisor told me she appreciated my scent-stopping efforts and that there was no longer a problem. Irina was right, again!

Back to the chatty IT guy.

When I told him no, that I was not dating anyone, he asked if I had been on Clash.com. IT Guy said he had just proposed to the love of his life, whom he had met on Clash. Furthermore, both of his brothers had met their wives on Clash. He offered to help me create the "perfect profile". This was a pretty compelling offer, so I agreed. Then IT Guy reiterated that he would help me, but first I had to go out on a date with one of his friends, a lawyer and medical writer for a pharmaceutical company. They were both members of this guys' group that met weekly. His friend was older than me, but he didn't say how much older. It all seemed harmless, so I was still game. Turns out, the guys in his group had dating rules. Of course, they did. Why was it never easy?

We had to email first, then after three emails, we could talk on the phone. Only after two to four phone chats, would a full-on date be acceptable. However, If I agreed to go on a double date, we could skip the phone chats and go straight to meeting, on said double date. The other couple would be another guy from this heavily regulated group and that guy's lucky lady friend. Half-jokingly, I asked if I could get a copy of the rules. "Is there a laminated facsimile I could carry around?"

The idle chit chat had quickly escalated. It all sounded exhausting. It also left me with one burning question: What's a guys' group? I've heard of guys getting together for fantasy football, poker, book clubs, fight clubs... But this crew, with Hammurabi's Code for dating, left me perplexed. And I still wasn't connected to the right printer.

Mister Confused Turtleneck sent the first e-mail. It contained footnotes. That was different. I had never received a personal email with footnotes, how unique! Then this: "Considering what you do for a living, I thought it would be amusing to share with you the fact that, when I was a child, I was scared of our family pharmacist. He was a pedophile. Looking forward to hearing from you!"

DEAR. GOD.

"So, you associating pharmacists with pedophilia is not the ideal situation. Unique, but not ideal. Yikes!" I replied. I shared that I have never met a man with his name before and that it makes me think of that song from the movie *Juno*. He had not seen *Juno*.

"Frankly, I assumed I'd live and die never hearing my name in a verse. It doesn't really rhyme well. $50 says I can name what you just tried to rhyme it with." I didn't take his wager.

Frankly, I didn't have time to rhyme, what with all the other foreign things he had referenced, asked about, or requested that I click on and respond to. That rhyme would just have to become another mystery I'd learn to live with. Mostly I was just confused about why he thought songs had to rhyme.

The next couple of emails he sent contained references to movies and tv shows I have never seen and to music I was not familiar with. He also asked more questions which included links I had to click on and watch before I could answer, and then more links to questions with instructions to choose one to answer and reply with my response. It was like a bad game show, with no grand prize or even nifty consolation prizes, and also terrible banter.

"So … how do you like being a pharmacist? Do you ever get that crew from Drugstore Cowboy in there faking seizures and what-not? Is Mort Goldman your hero?" he implored.

I had never seen Drugstore Cowboy. I added the movie to my Netflix queue and bumped it up to number one, but this was back when Netflix mailed you DVDs, so it took me days to fully comprehend the reference. I had to Google Mort Goldman and then watch a few episodes of *Family Guy* to see if he was, in fact, my hero.

Mister Ghost had introduced me to Netflix. At the time, it was mind blowing. He held up this red envelope, "They mail it to your house and there's no late fee!" he explained, rocking my world. If you grew up renting VHS tapes and DVDs, even while you questioned this new reality, you embraced it with gusto. I could not wait to get my own account and have three DVDs shipped to me all at once, forever.

Back to these insane emails. He sent a link to askmen.com (I know I was shocked too, that was a real website), saying, "For fun, why don't you pick a question from the list here." Before I knew it, I was printing out all his emails, conducting independent research, and flushing so much time down the toilet that I had to recruit help. My coworker, Susan, the math-major-turned-pharmacist, was assisting me in between work calls. It was like we were decoding a secret message and then once we figured it out, that was just the beginning, I still had to respond to him.

When I told him what music I listened to, he responded with, "I get Kings of Leon confused with Fountains of Wayne, and likewise with The Strokes and The White Stripes." What?! I had to read that sentence a few times. I knew he was older, but this made him sound like an out of touch uncle.

"I'm getting the feeling you are older than me. May I ask how old you are?" He was 10 years older than me. I couldn't wrap my head around what a phone conversation would be like, so I asked the IT Guy if I could invoke the double date rule, thus bypassing the phone conversations. He affirmed my invocation.

Our first date also coincided with my mother getting a new psychic. "If he doesn't have blue eyes, don't even bother," Mom said, passing along a message from her latest psychic friend. The date ended up being a single after all, just the two of us meeting on a rainy Friday night at P.F. Chang's. It already sounds depressing, doesn't it? IT Guy and his fiancée couldn't make it. I had gotten to a one-on-one dinner without having any phone conversations. This felt like a win until we sat down and he had absolutely nothing to say to me.

He was sitting there in a turtleneck and black sports jacket, both hands clutching an almost finished brown liquor drink. Fashion convention dictates that trends will come back around. For instance, turtlenecks are currently (not then) back in style, but there was nothing fashionable about this man's turtleneck. The black fabric clinging to his neck aged him. He did not have blue eyes. I was grateful for this because if he had had blue eyes, it would have freaked me out. Thankfully, this was just an old man in a turtleneck staring at me; not my one and only true love.

We were both dressed in all black ensembles. I had on a short-sleeved, velour midi-dress from a thrift store, paired with a large belt, cowboy boots, large purse, and trench coat. We looked like we came from a funeral and we were so bereft that we couldn't speak. My hair was down and straightened, which felt like a complete waste of time on this rainy night. It was definitely on its way back to frizzy and wavy. Time for a hair tie!

Once, with Mister Ghost, I had washed my hair and let it air dry while we were at breakfast at Breadman's in Chapel Hill, a casual place where I felt welcome in a t-shirt and clean but unstyled hair. Halfway through breakfast, Mister Ghost randomly asked if I had a hair tie so that I could do something about my hair. He said my hair was in a state where it was bothering him and he assured me that if I could see my hair, it would bother me too. After that, I never left home without multiple ways to corral my hair.

I tied my hair up, and was still waiting for Mister Confused Turtleneck to speak. Silence. Not even a corny opener like, "If you were a pirate, which shoulder would your parrot stand on?" My youngest sister, Megan, told me about this line and its corresponding shoulder touching, so that the person asking the question could use it to get their arm around your shoulders. It was time to bring out my heart-to-heart conversation cards from the pack I picked up at Walmart for a dollar around Valentine's Day.

I have never figured out how to manage awkward silences, so I make it even more uncomfortable by bringing out the cards. I'm fully aware that they're a crutch. I'm just horrible at small talk. The worst. My good friends Sarah and Curtis effortlessly maneuver through a party making friends by asking the exact right questions and selecting the perfect small talk topics. I worked with Sarah and we lived fairly close to each other, so we ended up carpooling to work-related events. I attached myself to Sarah and her husband in the hopes that one day I would learn the art of small talk. After watching Curtis in action for several hours one night, I asked if he would make his own conversation cards for me. He just laughed and shook his head. Hopeless.

"If you could have any pet, what would it be and why?" I asked, after flipping over a card from the deck.

"A monkey," he said, almost instantaneously.

"Um, you're also supposed to tell me why," I gently reminded him.

"I was at a rodeo and there was a dog with a monkey on its back running around. Something spooked the dog and it tried to escape. In the process, the dog killed the monkey. But the dog didn't know what else to do after it calmed down, so it went back to running in circles with this dead money on its back," he calmly explained.

I had follow-up questions.

"Why would this make you want a monkey as a pet?"

"Mmmaybe this didn't happen to me in real life. Maybe I saw it in a movie. I have trouble distinguishing what has happened to me in real life versus what I see in movies, sometimes." He laughs.

Does anyone know what horrific movie this dead monkey scene is from? I couldn't tell if he was messing with me, so I took the opportunity to bring up the pedophile statement from his email, "Was that in a movie or real life?" It seemed like an important question to ask. He just looked at me and smiled. I got up and headed to the bathroom, leaving my trench coat, umbrella, and purse at the table.

Heading back to the table, I passed him in the hallway and I was shocked that he had left the table and all my things. He gave me a high-five as I passed him.

"Tag, you're it!"

All my possessions were still at the table. I have never, ever had anyone think it was ok to leave the table while the other person is in the bathroom. You take turns. This guy was obviously raised by wolves. I was speechless, but put away the conversation cards. We sat in silence, eating.

"Tell me more about this guys' group you're in, " I said, speaking for the first time since he had tagged me. He didn't offer much, but I wasn't willing to let this go yet. I mentioned that the other day my friends and I had gotten together at my house to hang out. We had food and wine and made flowers out of tissue paper while listening to the Frank Sinatra station on XM Satellite Radio. Crafty spent her paycheck on a massive amount of tissue paper and taught us all how to make these fluffy and colorful paper flowers with pipe cleaners as stems.

"Is this something your guys' group does?"

He looked me in the eyes and smiled, again. No witty reply, just more staring.

Mister Confused Turtleneck walked me to my car after we paid separately. I try to slide into the driver's seat as fast as possible to avoid the sneak-attack-kiss and any potential awkwardness. I yelled goodnight over my shoulder and didn't look back. He followed up the next day with a text saying that he had a nice time and he wanted to hang out again. I would have never thought he had a good time if he had not told me. There were no clues. I texted back saying I wished him the best and that I simply was just not the girl for him. When I received his text, the day after our date, I was in Charlotte wedding dress shopping with one of my good friends, Bernadette, and her mother. His text prompted me to recount the highlights of our date while straddling the arm of the couch in the dressing room, waiting for Bernadette to appear in the next dress. We all laughed. It sounded even more absurd as I recounted it: the dead monkey, the high five on the way to the bathroom. But then, as I was discussing the use of my silly conversation cards with Bernadette's mother, I could not have felt more immature, so I abruptly stopped talking and left out the part that he had also lost his grasp on reality.

Bernadette's mother has one of the most soothing Southern voices I have ever heard. She looked at my sad face, smiled, and said, "I want to hear more about your dates." It made me smile. It was the perfect thing to say.

For years I slept under a framed quote, "Starlight, Starbright, Where the heck is Mister Right?" I thought it was funny, but one day my sister Katie told me that she decided it was probably bad luck to sleep under it. I had not met Mister Right, so I decided she was probably right, as usual, and I stuck something else in the pretty, blue, distressed frame.

"Was it really horrible, or a reality check?" asked Mister IT after I regaled him with date details. Despite it not being the best experience, I felt like I had successfully stuck my toe into the online dating pool and I was ready to get on Clash and see what else was out there. But I wasn't going it alone.

I convinced my two single friends, Crafty and SDH, to dive in with me by confidently assuring them that Mister IT would help us every step of the way, and then pointed out how well it worked for him and his brothers. We will be fine.

When I told Mister IT that it was finally time for Clash, he said, "I knew you would resort to it. Remember, be honest and weed out the trash. Mention the dogs. They are a big part of your life, as well as your family. Most guys will get the point."

One night at our favorite local coffee shop, Crafty, SDH, and I worked on our online dating profiles. We consulted one another on what pictures to post, what our taglines should be, and gave one another final approval once it all looked perfect. It took hours. We happily toasted each other with beers and coffees when we were all done. We took a moment to soak it all in, recognizing just how good it felt to be officially "out there" and available for online dates. We were so proud. It was going to be awesome!

We took pictures to commemorate the occasion, and I updated my Facebook status. Crafty, SDH, and I were all out there together, three worms on hooks.

In the beginning of our online dating journey, we decided to meet for a drink and consultation with our mutual friend Evan. We needed all the help we could get. Evan was online dating and he told us it was simple: "It's a numbers game! You just need to date as many people as possible." This was literally all he said because he had to get to a date.

In the interest of saving time, Crafty suggested at the end of our dates we could just text each other the number of hearts we felt while on it. It actually was a more long-drawn-out conversation specifically about Zelda hearts. We decided this would be our rating system, but, between Crafty, SDH and I, Crafty was the only one who played Zelda and she couldn't remember the number of maximum Zelda hearts. The point is, we were excited, and had one last drink before heading home. I can still see us, all smiles, and prepared to meet the loves of our lives. Boy, were we stupid.

Six

Mister Cat

Chapel Hill, NC circa 2009

In my experience, having friends set you up means that they have another single friend they also love and even though you have nothing in common besides the fact that you are both single, they want you to meet, fall in love, and marry. No biggie!

My friend and former coworker Heidi told me she knew this really great guy. He was so great that she wasn't sure she wanted to set him up with me. OUCH. She apologized for saying that later. But anyway, she had hyped him up so much that it made me curious. She had brought him up a few times when we spoke about my dating life, and it was like she was dangling this carrot. *I got him, the perfect guy, but I don't think I will set you two up. Wait, did I mention how great my single, male friend is? Oh wait, never mind.*

What did she really think of me? That was the question. All this hesitation made it perfectly clear.

"I would be interested in going out on a date with him, if you will let me," I said, finally.

She never actually said what made him so great. She called him Cat. It has something to do with his actual name and a cartoon cat from the silent film era. He already had a nickname, perfect. Mister Cat, the mysterious and rumored-to-be-wonderful man that I didn't deserve to be introduced to, awaited me!

She said that Mister Cat attended the last dinner party she'd thrown and we had been quickly introduced. I didn't remember. She also shared that he used to work where I currently work. I immediately started to ask around the office. One of my other coworkers and good friends, Weiderman, was also trying to set me up with this other pharmacist we worked with who was actively and aggressively pushing his way into my life. This included asking me to walk with him during our lunch break every day. We will call him Mister Clueless. He was tall, bespectacled, boringly business-casual, and in his own world 100% of the time. I had started out walking with him *and* Weiderman during lunch, but then she got too busy to walk and it was just the two of us. I don't know what he did to the office administrative assistant Peggy, but she got upset when she saw us walking together and pulled me aside one day and said, "Why are you walking with that man who walks like he has a giant stick up his ass?" I laughed because it was true and I had no answer for her. Why *was* I still walking with him? I would have rather been car-napping.

When I told Mister Clueless that I was going to have to pass on the walk and take a car nap instead, he told me that he was going to sit on the roof of my car and stare at me until I woke up and walked with him. Thankfully, he was always full of empty threats.

Car-napping is something Irina taught me. She had a pillow in her car and would put it in front of her as she sat in the driver's seat, in the parking lot, hugging it as she slept. For my car naps, I like to roll down the windows, push my seat back, close my eyes, and after 15 minutes, I truly feel like a new person. My body got so used to car naps that on days when my car was getting an oil change, I would ask to rent out my coworkers' cars to nap. They would ask the same of me. We were a small community of car-nappers and we all looked out for each other. I always parked in the same spot at work, in a shady corner away from other cars. My special spot, combined with a hot pink Piggly Wiggly sticker on the back window, made my car unmistakable. My coworker Renee had her own unique way of car-napping. Renee would open the doors of her car and lay across the back seat with her legs hanging out. Peggy would get so worried when it got hot in the summer and I was still car-napping every day she would yell after me as I walked out for my nap, "You better be careful because one of these days you are going to wake up dead!" One of my most treasured birthday presents is a tag from a mattress showroom that Renee gave me that says "Day Sleeper".

Mister Clueless was no match for the lure of the car-nap. When I had been dating Mister Loner (who you will be introduced to later), Mister Clueless told me that he knew Mister Loner wasn't social, so he would be happy to be my date for any and all events. I had to gently share with him that Mister Loner would not go for that plan, but thank you so much for offering. When Mister Clueless started seriously dating this nurse (we will call her Nurse Clueless), I thought it was finally safe to accept an invitation for a drink. I was just tired of putting it off. All I knew about Nurse Clueless was that she was a nurse and had a very regimented way of eating that was getting in the way of Mister Clueless' dining out and socializing.

I showed up for drinks and made it clear I would just have one drink and then had to meet my family for dinner. As I was finishing my martini, his girlfriend walked in and glared at me. I finally understood that phrase, *if looks could kill*. She wanted me to die a million different painful ways. He did not mention that she would be joining us or, apparently, mention me to her. They had been dating almost a year, they both were happy, she said, while inserting other fun facts about their relationship into her monologue. I probably should not have used the phrase "I know" so many times because that just seemed to make her angrier.

For our next encounter, Mister Clueless brought her as his date to an art show I was hosting at my house. I had just purchased a townhome and, instead of a traditional housewarming, I threw an art show for one of my coworker's wives who is an artist. My good friends Sarah and Curtis were my co-hosts and we served a wide variety of dips (the theme of the soiree was "Dip into Art"). It became an excuse to not only showcase a very talented artist but have my family, friends, and coworkers gather in my new home. Mister Clueless and his girlfriend were the first to arrive. It was awkward. She ended up leaving early, by herself. Mister Clueless stayed the entire time. He introduced himself to everyone, including my parents. Mister Loner was at "Dip into Art" too but he parked himself in the corner of the kitchen between the punch bowl and a vodka bottle. No one met Mister Loner that night, but everyone met Mister Clueless. This party was also the last straw for Mister Loner. Spending the entire evening by the punch bowl made him realize he could not pretend who he was anymore. After confidently telling me we would clean up together, he ended up fleeing on his bike after the party and broke up with me the next day (updates on this later.)

Soon after, Nurse Clueless started working at my office. My coworker Mike sat next to me, and in between us we had an automatic candy dispensing machine that we kept stocked with M&Ms. (Get it?!Mike & Mary!) Mike offered Nurse Clueless some candy and she just said she knew all about our machine and she wasn't interested. She then literally turned on her heels and walked off. Mike looked at me confused and said "Well, that's a fine how-do-you-do!" I was forced to explain who she was dating. Mister Clueless was a daily visitor to our candy dispenser but he never said hello to Mike. It drove Mike nuts. No matter how many times I told him he was lucky not to be acknowledged by Mister Clueless, he still complained. Mister Clueless was eating all our M&Ms. The least he could've done was thank Mike. Mister Clueless never thanked Mike but he did buy us more M&Ms, so maybe he wasn't totally clueless.

As It turns out, Mister Clueless also knew an eligible Mister named Cat (Improbable, but somehow true). They had worked together for years on the same project. Mister Clueless was also a huge fan of this Mister Cat, mostly, but had some concerns about me dating him; concerns he inappropriately shared with me in the hallway after work one day. I was leaving the office with all my bags when he stopped me right in between the break room and the bathroom, in full view of all of our colleagues.

My coworkers make fun of me because I bring so many bags to work. I have a bare minimum of three bags I lug around on a daily basis. They're full of all my products; thus, my nickname, Produx. There is always my purse; a bag with my breakfast, lunch, beverages and snacks; and then a third miscellaneous bag full of essentials such as paperwork, Duck Tape, magazines, books, deodorant, toothpaste, toothbrush, hairspray …

Mister Clueless had to tell me that this Mister Cat was substantially older and had been married before. I put all my bags down and thanked him for his concern and reassured him that I didn't want to get married or have kids, so maybe we would be the perfect match. "But are you sure?" he insisted. "I mean, positive, you don't want to get married or have kids? You may just think that right now but you're young and things might change, and then it's too late because you're already in love and in a relationship with an old man who doesn't want kids. So, think about whether you should even go out with him at all." [Pause for a giant eye roll.]

I have had this marriage-and-kids conversation with literally every person I know, plus some strangers. It takes people off guard when I tell them that I do not want marriage and kids. People do not accept it, no matter how confidently I say it. I have been told countless times, "Eventually you'll get married and have kids. It's inevitable." I smile back and sheepishly say, "Maybe you're right." It's the only way to get them to stop. It's exhausting. I wish I could just point to the beautifully framed "Living in Sin" cross-stitch that I have lovingly arranged with a ceramic hand giving the middle finger in my living room. Please see exhibit A. It speaks for itself. No more questions!

When I was younger, I didn't think I had a choice and that marriage would eventually happen to me. Growing up in a suburban neighborhood in Northeast Philadelphia, where everyone went to the same Catholic Church and all the kids went to the same parochial school, I was surrounded by a certain lifestyle and I thought that meant I would marry and have several children. To this day, my father will tell you that the entire point of life is getting married and having kids. I can still see the disappointment and anger in his face when I told him, "Well, I guess my life will be pointless then."

Flashback: October 30, 1998: It was my 19th birthday and I remember being shocked that my Aunt Elaine had called me sobbing. She first wished me a Happy Birthday but it was quickly followed by her telling me how happy she was that I wasn't getting married. It shocked me to hear her crying. Her sadness was completely foreign to me. I had never seen her not laughing, let alone not happily telling stories about her life. It was the best. When my Aunt Pat, my mom's oldest sister, and my Aunt Elaine, the second oldest, were around for family dinners or holidays, they would drink white wine. Aunt Pat's white wine required ice cubes, and they would tell stories that made motherhood sound like a laugh a minute. I could not wait for them to start telling these stories and I always wanted one more. Aunt Pat and Aunt Elaine each had four children. Aunt Elaine had a favorite story about her cherubic, youngest child whom she took everywhere, including to bowling night with her foul-mouthed bowling team. With her curly blond locks and blue eyes, the child would tell her siblings, "You wait here, you bastards," as she left the car and went into the store with her mother.

My favorite story stars a robed Aunt Elaine running chasing after her two young sons who were being thrown in a police paddy wagon. Aunt Elaine jumped into the wagon and started pulling her sons out while yelling at the cops. Then she looked around and realized she knew other kids in the paddy wagon. Aunt Elaine pulled out several more kids and announced they would all be going with her. The cops just let her go with the pint size gang. Why they were rounding up all these kids was never clear to me. Why would they just let her take the goonies with her? I felt like I had some insight into the last question.

Aunt Elaine, Aunt Pat, and my mother are all stunningly gorgeous women. I know I'm biased, but really, their looks are how people know them. This will put their beauty in perspective: My Aunt Pat's husband dated Grace Kelly before he dated Aunt Pat. Although Aunt Pat looked similar to Grace Kelly, Aunt Pat was even more beautiful. In college, when I was trying to figure out love and relationships, I asked my father how he knew my mother was *the one*. He quickly responded that "she was the most beautiful woman I ever saw. So, I dated her and married her, that's it—not that complicated."

When beautiful women are described to me, it all sounds the same, so I won't put you through that. But, for me, it's their eyes that set them apart. I didn't realize the full magnitude of my mother's palest-of-the-pale blue eyes until she was picking me up from a middle school pool party. I overheard all the guys in my class—the ones who made harsh, judgmental comments about my own looks—talking so adoringly and specifically about how beautiful my mom's eyes were. I was genuinely shocked to hear them using these words. When I looked over at them, they were just staring at her, after she had taken her sunglasses off. Then one day in the lunchroom I overheard some of these same male middle schoolers ask each other if they thought I was "cute." I walked away, never officially hearing the verdict. I was trying not to care what they thought.

There was also a summer break when we went to Maine and then New York City as a family. While I was wandering around The Metropolitan Museum of Art, straying just far enough from my family for strangers to think I was not with them, a man came up to me and asked if I had been in a laundromat in Bar Harbor, Maine, last Thursday night. I said yes, startled. Before I could ask him anything else, he said he was there too, and he remembered us because he remembered my mom. Then he walked away.

Anyway, I told my Aunt Elaine that I too was happy I wasn't getting married. It seemed like a total and complete impossibility to my 19-year-old self. Then I asked her why she was so upset. She wouldn't tell me specifics, only that she had gotten married on her 19th birthday. This didn't explain the tears, but it spoke volumes to me about marriage. This teary birthday conversation was a wake-up call and the first time I saw a crack in the perfect family façades all around me. How was I going to get more insight? My first thought was: when do I graduate from the kid's table at Thanksgiving? That must be when they discuss all the important stuff, while we are all stuck at the kids' table. I would never find out. Little did I know I would still be sitting at the kid's table in my 30's. I know, it was a gift.

My family moved from Philly to Carrboro, North Carolina, when I was a freshman in high school. My environment drastically changed. I traded a Quaker school for public school and suddenly lived in an area that has the most PhDs per square mile than anywhere in the U.S. I gradually saw different ways you can have a family.

Cara, my best friend in high school, had physicians for parents and she and her two siblings had a housekeeper and nanny for most of their childhood. It seemed as if her mother had it all. She had even kept her maiden name when she married, which, at that time, I didn't even know was possible.

During my middle school years, the sitcom character Murphy Brown decided to keep her baby and not marry the father. Her choice managed to upset people in real life. Dan Quayle said Murph was sending the wrong message. But the message was not for him! I received it loud and clear.

But what ended up really shattering my idea of a conventional family was meeting my coworker Daphne who was a single mother to two adopted children. She went to Kazakhstan with a translator to adopt them. She hadn't met the right partner, but she knew she wanted to be a mother. It was supposed to be just one baby but when she got there, she said she couldn't leave the other behind. I was so impressed by her. Not only did she get exactly what she wanted, but she made the struggle look effortless. Her kids turned out to be equally as impressive. Daphne's twelve-year-old daughter, in her spare time, designed and made a hat for her pet hedgehog out of construction paper. How did she know the perfect accessory for a hedgehog is a wide-brimmed pink hat with a flower on top? I have no idea but the results were adorable! Daphne's son came with her to an art show at my house and he described the art and what he thought it meant better than most of the adult guests.

After Daphne and I had become friends, I had a vivid nightmare. My parents took it upon themselves to adopt two baby girls for me to raise completely on my own because, as my nightmare parents told me, "You seemed so enamored with the idea." They then walked away, leaving me holding these two chubby white babies dressed in matching white lace gowns and bonnets—all three of us just staring at each other as I mentally thanked them for not crying.

The idea of having my own children went out the window during the barbaric 27-hour birth of my Goddaughter. There was a moment when I was holding one leg and Carmen's husband was holding the other leg, and the doctor, between us, looked at me and said, "I think we need the vacuum."

"Sir, despite appearances, I don't work here," I responded, horrified. We managed to also wedge the co-Godmother in the room, Irina, by hiding her behind the curtain. We were over the maximum number of visitors allowed, but everyone was so busy and Irina is so tiny that she just hid every time a nurse or doctor entered the room. The word vacuum was still hanging in the air when I looked at the curtains and saw Irina's wide, concerned eyes. She mouthed, "Vacuum???" and pantomimed vacuuming the floor through a crack in the curtains. Our 8-pound 5-ounce Goddaughter was born with some complications from the shoulder dystocia she experienced during her birth, but she is now happy and healthy, and I am very happy to remain Aunt Mary for the rest of my life.

Mister Cat was 15 years older than me but he didn't look like an old man (maybe that was because his Facebook profile picture was him as a baby). I picked the local restaurant Lantern for our first date because the bar area is my favorite place on Earth, and if Mister Cat didn't live up to the hype, I could at least enjoy an ice cold, bone dry, extra dirty vodka martini, or two, and delicious steamed dumplings.

If I can help it, I would rather not be sober and starving on a date. SDH and I would go to Lantern so much we knew the name of the MAC lip color our favorite bartender wore, and once she gave us free bowls of popcorn to go with our martinis. In addition to our martinis, we always ordered dumplings and warm chocolate cake— we were predictable, and the bar was predictably perfect. There is a back door you can enter from the alley and it is the best feeling to enter that way because you emerge directly into a cozy, dimly lit lounge from a secret passageway. It is impossible to make a cool entrance while fighting your way through a heavy curtain, but once you break through, it's worth it, if just for the glossy, black, textured walls and framed cat art. It never changed. Ah, home.

With Mister Cat, we went through the main entrance, which was bright, open, and white, and then made our way to the back. I didn't know him well enough to take him in the magic back way. Maybe it was nerves or the red lighting behind the tables, but he was very red every time I looked at him, like he was under a food warming lamp, and he didn't seem to have anything interesting to say—at all. Why did people think he was such a great guy? I didn't see even a glimmer.

There was a lot of staring at the menu followed by a lot of talk of his ex-wife who was now with someone else who happened to be a female. I realize that this could be an interesting topic, but he seemed like he was still processing it, so it was more like a therapy session. I didn't ask questions, I just let him talk. I thought we would have more to talk about, so I didn't even think to bring the conversation cards—a date-mistake I would never make again. The only thing we had in common was the place he used to work was the place I was currently trying to survive every day. Mister Cat was a total snooze fest and besides still being Facebook friends who don't wish each other happy birthday, I never heard from him again. I learned from Facebook that shortly after we went out, he met a woman who he is currently married to. I hope his real life is as happy as his wife's Facebook posts make it seem.

I learned a valuable lesson that night. If I like my friend and my friend likes my potential date, that does not automatically mean I will like my potential date. It is like the transitive property of dating, and unlike in math, the transitive property does not always work when it comes to dating. How deceptive!

Anyway, this was the perfect end to a date. It was clear to both of us that we never wanted to go through it again and there would be no forced goodbyes or trying again or anything. It became a vague memory of a date that happened, so I could say that I was trying, that I was meeting other single, eligible people who my friends recommended. I was putting myself out there and, yes, love is a motherfucking battlefield.

Seven

Mister Vintage Horse Trough

Carrboro, NC Circa late 2008

I received a direct message on Facebook from a guy I am not Facebook friends with.

"Mary,
I am a friend of Shannon and George. If you are interested, my
other friend would love to meet you. This is a bit strange I know. His
pictures are on my site. Here's his email.

Merry Christmas.

Walter"

I was pleasantly surprised. He was ruggedly cute in army gear and surrounded by soldiers in some far-off land abundant with sand and camels. I IM'd Weiderman (Shannon) at work and told her to meet me at my cubicle because I was looking up her guy on Facebook. Feeling optimistic, as I shared the pic of uniformed young men with my cubicle mate Allyson, Weiderman strolled up: "Oh no, it's not the guy in front. He's married. Remember it's Walter's Facebook account, our former neighbor, I think it's that little guy beside him." Naturally.

The man that Shannon, George, and Walter wanted to set me up with was cute, a nurse, and formerly in a special operations unit for the army. Walter's friend was single and I was single. It was another classic example of well-meaning friends trying to set me up with the only other single person they know. In spite of what I had just learned about the transitive property of dating, I still decided to go on this date. He seemed interesting and I was curious. I had never been on a date with anyone in the army before.

We sent some emails to set up a phone call. When I asked him how his day was, he told me his job was top secret (to this day I don't know a single thing about his job), so he could not tell me about it. OK, no problem, my work is in a call center, so I can easily pivot from work talk to books and movies—the bread and butter of my life.

He doesn't read books OR watch movies. I was stunned.

For more than a decade I have attended the Sundance Film Festival in Park City, Utah, where I have a dear friend. It is my favorite vacation: a week of going to the movies! How can someone not read ANY books or watch ANY movies? I had no idea what we were supposed to talk about, perhaps all the things we did not have in common.

"What do you do for fun?" I asked incredulously. "I enjoy antiquing and skeet shooting," he replied.

Now we were getting somewhere! What, exactly, was an army nurse based in Fayetteville going antiquing for? I braced myself.

"Vintage horse troughs," he said.

I love to shop and go to a variety of thrift and vintage stores, but, sadly, I have never encountered a vintage horse trough. Maybe this would broaden my thrift store horizons?

I was relieved when he explained that skeet shooting involved shooting at clay and not animals. Although, it sounded like a gateway to actual hunting. Truth be told, I am not all that into guns. One time I was surrounded by guns. I wasn't in any danger, just in the house of one of my former pharmacy school preceptors, THE preceptor. I had never heard the term *preceptor* before pharmacy school. A preceptor is supposed to be an experienced practitioner who provides supervision during clinical practice. But, outside of THE preceptor, in my experience a preceptor was a pharmacist who either pawned me off on their colleagues or completely left me alone to fend for myself behind the high counter. In their defense, pharmacists are extremely busy, so I get not wanting someone slowing you down even if you are getting paid to mentor them. (We will get back to Mister Vintage Horse Trough in a second).

The preceptor's dad was a gun collector and he had passed away and left his son the entire collection. The preceptor had just brought the collection back from California and the entire perimeter of his guest room was lined with large, gun-shaped duffel bags. Homey, right?

There was no bed or dresser or any other furniture, just your typical bonus room filled with bags of guns. As I stood at the door, taking it all in, he was telling me that he didn't know what he was going to do with them, but he felt like he had to keep them because it was the only thing he had of his dad's. It didn't feel right. This Michael J. Fox doppelganger in a white lab coat came home to a room of guns after a hard day of pharmacy-ing?

He asked if I wanted to see the guns. I quickly declined. He then asked me if I wanted to see the gun he kept loaded in a safe in his bedroom. When I politely declined that too, he still brought it out to show me. He had been drinking beer for most of that afternoon and evening, so the last thing I wanted to see in his hands was a loaded gun. It made the preceptor laugh to see me so uncomfortable. This all happened after we got back from an impromptu dinner out. I thought I was just there to learn how to change my oil. He was a mechanic in his previous life, and he said he would teach me. I hadn't anticipated walking into his kitchen full of trash and dishes—and that smell. When he saw my face, he said his girlfriend was out of town. I never expected to be going to dinner with him.

He ended up breaking into his own house after dinner because he had locked us out. The oil change lesson came the following morning after he slept on the couch and I in his bed, after he insisted. He woke me up to tell me that his girlfriend was on her way back home, and he started stripping the sheets off the bed with me still in it. I was there to learn how to change my oil, seriously, so I wasn't leaving until we had the lesson. I didn't care who was coming home, especially since I had done nothing wrong. I never even touched him. As far as I was concerned, being as young and dumb as I was at the time, we were just hanging out.

I learned some valuable lessons from this oil change lesson that almost wasn't. If someone offers to teach you how to change your oil at their house, they probably have no intention of actually teaching you this life skill. It's a trap to get you to their house/garage. Being side by side, under a car with someone is a strangely intimate experience. And changing oil is something I will pay someone else to do for the rest of my life. I also made a mental note to always remember to carry either contact lens solution, contacts, or a pair of glasses in my bag. When you are alone with a man, I have found it to be vital that you are able to see, not to mention that putting your contacts in a makeshift solution will only add to the uncomfortableness the morning after when you try to put them back in.

Several days after the gun show/oil change, the preceptor and I were driving down the highway in his jeep when he told me he had feelings for me. We had just had dinner with my friends and he asked to drive me home so it was just the two of us. I rolled down the window and puked.

The puke ended up streaking down the side of the jeep. (This won't be the last time this happens). Apparently if you tell me you have feelings for me, I puke. Totally normal.

"That wasn't exactly the response I was looking for," he said, after a short pause. In my defense, just a month ago he was my pharmacy preceptor. I really did not see our emotional entanglement and the consequent blowing of chunks coming.

THE preceptor was always around me. As my preceptor, he had invited me to hear him give a talk and have a drink after. I thought he had extended the invite because he was my preceptor and he wanted to educate me and make sure I wasn't going to kill anyone on his watch. It really didn't seem odd to me.

Since I was his student, it may go without saying that he was older than me, 14 years or so older than me. Although he wasn't married, he shared with me that he was in a ten-year relationship with a woman he lived with. I did like him as a person, but I never thought of him in a romantic way because in my mind he was completely untouchable. Well, I was wrong.

I never responded to him telling me he had feelings for me because I didn't know what to say or how I felt about him. It was a shock when he called me the Saturday morning following his ignored declaration. I was sitting in the seat of the blood pressure machine next to the pharmacy counter at Eckerd, waiting for the pharmacist to arrive, when I looked down at my hot-pink Nokia cell phone. Who was calling me before 9am on a Saturday? With the old-school Nokia phones, you could not see who was calling; it just flashed "Call," so I picked up. It was THE preceptor calling to let me know that it was over with his girlfriend. All I could say was that I was at work and we hung up.

Ajay, my co-worker, looked at me concerned and asked if everything was ok. I told him what had happened and he just started laughing. I had told him all about THE preceptor and even though I thought there was no possibility of a relationship because of his long-term, live-in girlfriend, Ajay knew better. He told me to be careful and that maybe I don't need to always accept his invitations. He thought it was hilarious that I was so shocked. Ajay was going to have an arranged marriage but he thought he was in love with someone else who was also supposed to have an arranged marriage—not to him. He always told me he had "real problems" and envied my "white girl" dating freedoms.

When THE preceptor and I were able to talk, he explained that he never really loved his girlfriend of 10 years. He had "saved her" from her ex-husband who was an "alcoholic dwarf undertaker." Seriously?

Then THE preceptor said he was moving to Alaska and wanted me to come too. Alaska?! I was definitely not ready to move to Alaska, with or without him. Luckily, I did not have to make up an excuse. I already had plans. I promised my sister Katie and friend Monte that I would live with them in South Carolina. My sister found us a place to live a block away from the beach near Charleston and down the street from her boyfriend at the time. We were going to live by the shore and it was supposed to be for a year or two. (I ended up staying for 5 years, building a family of friends, and eventually completely losing control of my household). But I wasn't sure if I was making a mistake by not exploring this preceptor relationship further.

When I told my friend Sean about Alaska, he said we needed to meet at our usual bar and discuss. We spent hours talking about what it meant to fall in love and how you would know you were in love. I had been going into the field on rotations for pharmacy school in an area of North Carolina the school referred to as "Area L." THE preceptor was overseeing my rotations in the field. Sean said, well, now we finally know what that L stands for, "love!" As we laughed and talked and drank, we were sitting outside under a tree, so he could smoke when it started to rain. Everyone else went inside, but we were shielded by this giant tree, so we stayed outside sharing a cigarette in silence. The longer we sat, the more I realized that I was unusually calm, happy, and present. That's when everything became clear. I was definitely not in love with THE preceptor. This is when Sean became Mister Ring of Fire (more on that in a minute).

It wasn't until years later, when I found THE preceptor on Facebook, that I saw he is still in Alaska and calls it "heaven." I am not sure I would have called it the same.

Remember Mister Vintage Horse Tough? (I love a good tangent!) So, basically the only thing he and I could talk about were our dogs. He too was a dog owner and that is what all of his Facebook pictures consisted of: him, his dog, or him and his dog. Since we didn't live near one another, it was going to be awhile before we could meet. I had never attempted the conversation cards over the phone, but I was seriously thinking about it. When I would ask how his day was, he would tell me something vague like, "I jumped out of a plane today."

I have never jumped out of a plane, so I had lots of questions, but he was bored with this line of questioning because, to him, it was a training exercise he did all the time. He was jumping out of planes, saving lives, and I was in the training portion of my new job, which meant I was studying medications all day—not the subject matter of great work stories. In between talking on the phone and meeting for the first time, I landed in Park City for Sundance. While walking around one day, I saw a street sign that bore his last name. It is not a common name for a street, so I thought it was a sign of things to come and, more importantly, something we could talk about.

He knew that I liked hearing live music and there was a band he knew coming to the Cat's Cradle, which was near my house, so we had our first date all lined up. He would pick me up and we would have dinner across the street from the venue and then go to the show.

He did not prepare me for his truck. It was huge, loud, and had several giant flood lights on top of it—a car that is rarely, if ever, seen in environmentally-conscious Carrboro. It did not seem to fit on the roads or in any parking spots.

I am 5 feet 9 inches tall and I had to jump into and out of his truck. We finally found a spot to park that seemed legal and headed to dinner. He was very nice, but we just didn't have any areas of *mutual penetration*. This is a term Crafty came up with one night while we were out drinking (we had progressed from Zelda hearts to this new concept, mutual penetration, but kept the cocktails). The gist of it is: A romantic couple must have at least one thing you enjoy doing together so that when things get rough, or you need to reconnect, you can go back to your *thing*—your point of mutual penetration. It's a handy term, but I have learned that you can't say it out loud in all spaces or with the corresponding hand motions Crafty developed, impromptu, to nonverbally represent the phrase: basically, two fingers coming together suggestively. It was hard not to turn heads.

Mister Vintage Horse Trough and I went to the show and it was nice because we were not able to talk. We just stood side by side with our beers and enjoyed the music. The only time he spoke to me was to point out that another woman had on a dress and cowboy boots like me, but he said that I was wearing it better. Like I said, he was very nice.

I had on a vintage, velour, V-neck, short-sleeved dress with a giant, black belt and my black cowboy boots. He drove me home and all I was thinking about was avoiding the sneak-attack-kiss. As I mentioned before, I really hate the sneak-attack-kiss. I have closed doors in faces, spun around, put my hand up, anything to avoid this. I wasn't sure if his mind was in sneak-attack mode, but I didn't want to find out. So, before he even stopped the truck, I jumped out.

I thought maybe I had broken my ankles because it was such a long way down, but I had to do what I had to do. I was grateful it was dark as I did my best to hobble into my house. I was also grateful that I was wearing my black Justin cowboy boots for the jump—not heels. I don't think I would have survived otherwise. Mister Horse Trough jumps out of planes and I get injured jumping out of his slow-moving monster truck.

We shared nothing in common and clearly, I wasn't the girl for him. I shared that sentiment with him in a final follow-up email. It was the only time I ever offered a reason as to why I was not *the* girl to any of my dates. He agreed, but we remained Facebook friends and he sent me a few private messages asking for the name of the restaurant we had gone to and, later, to give me feedback on a show he'd attended at the Cradle. It left me wondering if he was recreating our date? Then he asked me for more music venue recommendations, but before that he congratulated me on being married.

I had been trying to prove to Mister Loner (who you will meet next) that you could put anything on Facebook and it didn't mean it was true. My little sister Megan's profile said she was married to one of her best friends, Emma, which I thought was a great idea. But when I tried to do the same with Monte, she never confirmed it. Instead of people thinking it was cute that I was married to one of my very best friends, it just said I was married but didn't list to whom. It created a lot of confusion and awkward congratulations.

"Actually, I'm not really married," I messaged him. "How do you apologize to someone about that? I'm glad to hear you're not ... um ... anyways ..." he replied.

"You don't need to apologize, I do, and I am sorry to put false information on my Facebook page, but I did have a reason, but it's a long story and it makes me seem crazier ... " "I've heard of people putting 'married' on their profiles, so you are not the only one and are not crazy," he continued, gentlemanly. "The reason I'm asking is that I've been seeing a girl and I was looking for different places to take her." I didn't respond.

About a year went by, then I got another message from him offering an extra last-minute ticket to a show at the Cradle. "Are you up for it??????????"

At this point it had been almost two years since our date, with little communication in between. I had never heard of the band, which hasn't stopped me in the past, but I wasn't sure why he was asking me. Did he just want someone to see concerts with? I was already deep in some weird pseudo- friendship-postdating situation with Mister Loner. The thought of adding Mister Vintage Horse Trough to that roster was not appealing. I wanted someone who had the potential to be more than a friend, so I declined the ticket. He never contacted me again and although he didn't say it, he was probably grateful he got away from a lying lunatic who jumped out of a moving truck for no reason.

Eight

Mister Loner

Carrboro, NC circa 2009

He was my very first Clash.com date. I bought a black tank-top and a gray and black, zebra print midi-skirt from Target to pair with my black cowboy boots. Mister Loner lived in Carrboro and claimed to be a musician, tall, and in a full-arm cast from a skateboarding accident. We met at Open Eye Cafe, a local coffee shop. When I arrived, I noticed after taking a seat outside that there was a tall man in a full-arm cast sitting inside at a table, alone, staring at his beer. It had to be him. We appeared to be in a standoff, err *sitoff*. Who was going to make the first move, inside or out?

I texted. I saw him read it, take a deep breath, and rise to come outside. As he sat down with his beer, he moved the table so it spilled most of my coffee. I didn't care because it was just a prop, but he really beat himself up over it. I should have helped him. The man only had one useful arm! I was already screwing up this meet-cute.

All I could think about was the "The Car Door Test" from the movie *A Bronx Tale*. Mister Ghost had put me through the test on one of our early dates and I had failed. It's when the male opens the car door and lets you in first and then the female is supposed to reach over and unlock his door or at the very least make sure it's unlocked. I know it's outdated but it's supposed to be a selfishness indicator. When I failed, Mister Ghost shamed me, saying that it showed what type of person I was. I vowed to change. I guess it's true that people don't actually change. I hadn't even thought to get up to help a one-armed man sit down with his beverage.

He started telling me the story of how he ended up in the giant cast. He sounded so pained. Mister Loner had skateboarded for 20 years and this injury forced him to decide to give it up. He was getting older and he could not go through or afford any more injuries, so this was the accident that made him retire from his passion. I felt his sadness as he related his woes, still dressed like a skateboarder.

Mister Loner is part of the first generation of aged skateboarders. As he was talking, I was thinking he must be around the same age as Tony Hawk, who, at the time, was still skateboarding. Retired football players, or any sports players I can think of, do not suit up in their old uniforms and go about town. But skaters do. I guess if that's how you dressed your whole life, why would you change? So here he was, Peter Pan wearing the uniform of his youth, indefinitely. All I could say was at least he found his passion and had it for 20 years. I was envious, and he was sitting there visibly upset about the symbolic finality of his injury.

His t-shirt read "BOLO" and featured a picture of a waving guy who resembled Waldo but without the signature red and white striped shirt and hat. I launched into a story of when I was in pharmacy school and still living in the dorms. There had been a sexual assault on campus, and on every door of every dorm there was a sketch of the assailant's face. Under his face was just one word, "BOLO."

"Watch out for BOLO ladies. Be safe!" my friends and I would shout to one another when we parted ways and headed back to our respective dorms. It wasn't until someone overheard us and explained, through her laughter, that the perp's name was not BOLO and that it stood for, "Be On The Lookout." We had no idea.

Mister Loner laughed at the story and said that for him it meant "B," as in the first letter of his name, plus "solo," as it is just him. He used to be in bands but it never panned out for him. He now performs as a solo musician under the name "Bolo" and the Waldo-looking dude on his t-shirt, that's supposed to be him. He is "B Solo." That should have been the only red flag I needed. He was showing me exactly who he was and instead of believing him, I was too busy batting away red flags.

He had come on our date with a picture of himself on his t-shirt. I posted this on Facebook to see what my friends and family thought. The majority just chalked it up to being quirky in Carrboro, but my sister Katie shamed me for being too judgmental. So what, the man has a t-shirt with his band name and likeness on it? Let him live! She thinks I am way too picky even though I tell her that the one thing I think you should be the pickiest about is who you date. Katie had made me feel bad for even posting this question, so I took it down and never told him about it.

I eventually got my own BOLO t-shirt. He gave it to me and made sure to tell me that his ex-girlfriend had designed it and it was the only one he had left. I wondered if she had also worn it. It was nowhere near my size but I graciously accepted it.

I will never forget the time Mister Ring of Fire announced, as we departed high school, that from here on out anyone we dated, we could also potentially marry. At the time, that statement blew my mind. It became my first "old-age-awareness moment." Marriage. The word makes me shudder. I had NEVER felt like the person I was sitting across from on a date was potential marriage material. This guy was no exception but here I was twelve years out of high school, sitting in front of a man in a full-arm cast who seemed to be fully depressed and wasn't trying to hide it on a first date. I found this refreshing! And, if I'm being fully honest, it was charming. Sigh.

At the end of the date, he walked me to my car. I felt ashamed for driving an SUV around Carrboro and I wanted to own up to it before we reached my car. Mister Loner had made it clear in his dating profile that he enjoyed riding his bike but not in tight shorts. He said the tight-short thing a few times and I wasn't sure why he kept mentioning it. I explained that I got my SUV when I was living in Charleston, which is called the Low Country for a reason, and that every time it rained, my route to work would flood. I hadn't realized how bad the flooding was until I was driving to work one Saturday morning in my Honda Civic and the water felt like it was up to my door handles. I panicked and called Sarah, the intern who was working with me that morning. She said, "Just go for it, and if you stall out, I will come get you." I made it, but after that terrifying experience I signed a lease for an SUV.

Mister Loner had ridden his bike to our date, so he was walking with his bike next to me and listening to me attempt to justify my SUV. I kept talking. I felt like he was the epitome of the environmentally conscious Carrboro local, but when I finally finished my confession, he just looked at me and smiled. He drives a pickup truck. He did feel the need to throw in that it was his brother's old work truck. I felt close to him already.

It wasn't until our second date, when we ended up at a bar at the end of the evening, that I saw him relaxed. He had a beer at Open Eye but at OCSC (Orange County Social Club) he was drinking bourbon and ginger ale. The way he ordered it made me think of an old Murphy Brown episode. Murph talked about how she could identify other alcoholics, since she was one, by how they ordered their specific drink and then how they looked at it like a life preserver. In middle school, when I saw the episode, I had no idea what it meant, but for some reason it stuck with me. That and a line Eldin has in the episode where Murphy gives birth and Eldin is talking into a camera directly to her unborn son: "Remember kid, nothing takes the place of authentic." Eldin had missed the birth because he had gone to Maryland to eat crab cakes. Anyway, I heard Murphy say the life preserver line in my head when I watched Mister Loner receive that drink.

He knew almost everyone at the bar and they addressed him by name or just by the letter B. He seemed to have a lot of friends and they were all in bands, some were in multiple bands. They asked me what instrument I played and I was so inspired being surrounded by all these musicians that I shared something I rarely do about how I used to play the violin. I still have the one I played in high school. My father is so convinced I will start playing again that he recently gave me another violin as a Christmas present. Now I have two violins that live in my closet.

"We could really use a violinist in our band," piped up one of Mister Loner's friends. I thought maybe this would be what prompted me to finally start playing again. Well, it wasn't. But that night I learned more about his past. His mother sent him to rehab when he was a teenager. Initially, I did not wave away this red flag but I told him that I thought we should just be friends. He agreed, but followed it up with, "Only if there is a chance we could be more than friends in the future?"

I knew that was a bad idea, but I felt like maybe it was an inevitability. It goes back to a line in the movie *When Harry Met Sally*. Billy Crystal's character says, "What I'm saying is—and this is not a come-on in any way, shape or form—is that men and women can't be friends because the sex part always gets in the way." I believed that line to be true, so I smiled and told him, "Yes, there is always a chance."

Shit. Who was I kidding? It was already happening.

I went home and cried. I can't explain why. It was like a pre-cry for all that was going to come; like I knew this was going to be painful. The next day I was hanging out with Kristen, one of my former pharmacy interns who was on-call for her job. I agreed to go on some errands with her so we could spend time together, and the first stop was Michaels. Kristen wanted to scrapbook her last vacation as a gift to her husband. I needed someone I trusted to talk me out of this burgeoning relationship cloaked in red flags. But Kristen was so overwhelmed by all the scrapbooking options at

Michaels that she was the one who started crying. She walked over to me with this giant pile of stickers, knowing that if she purchased all of them it would be the same cost as her vacation, but she couldn't choose. A stranger had to come over and talk her down.

"I've been there before, honey! There are a lot of stickers and it can be overwhelming. Let's just think about three specific activities that you want to focus on and get stickers for those," the helpful stranger offered as she put her arm around Kristen. She had clearly done this before. Maybe she worked as an undercover aisle counselor for Michaels? I wanted to ask her what to do about Mister Loner too, but we did not have that kind of time. Kristen was already headed to check out with half the number of stickers in her pile, and we could all hear the multiple phones stuffed in her purse buzzing. When you're on-call, you have to answer, even when having a Michaels meltdown. We had more errands to run and as Kristen was screaming TPN (Total Parenteral Nutrition) orders into the phone while we sped off to Target, I decided I was not going to waste her time with the inevitable.

Yes, I saw the red flags. Mister Loner presented me with each one, until there was a bouquet. I accepted them, put them in water, and, true to how I approach many-a-challenge, I daydreamed as we moved very slowly into a relationship.

Mister Loner ended up living down the street from me, so he would ride his bike, never wearing a helmet, to my house to hang out. My friend Lilli would text me when she saw him out and about in Carrboro on his bike and she always ended the text with, you should tell him that he really needs to wear a helmet. I never saw him with a helmet.

Proximity and convenience have helped along many doomed relationships. It felt like I was back in Philadelphia, living in our twin-home neighborhood that surrounded the Catholic school and church that everyone I knew attended. We, the neighborhood children, would set out every day after school on our bikes. We knocked on one another's front doors to see who could hang out. We rode our bikes everywhere and never chained them up, dropping them whenever we arrived at our destination. We never wore helmets.

Mister Loner used to chain his bike to the handrail in front of my townhome. I would hear the doorbell ring and then I'd look down from the little window by my door and see his utilitarian bike. My heart would race.

In the beginning it was a friendship and he would come over and we would cook and watch movies, TV shows, talk, or just drink together. I felt safe with him in the beginning. He seemed so sad and timid and spoke in this almost baby-like voice at times. Even though he seemed too timid for it, I knew better, and still feared the sneak-attack-kiss.

One evening, I went to his apartment and he cooked us dinner, carrot dogs. I love a hot dog, a regular hot dog, and a sauteed carrot masquerading as a hot dog just wasn't the same. After we dined on carrot dogs and potato wedges, we were sitting on his futon, side by side, and, instead of enjoying the moment, I fled. I was wearing a white, Gap V-neck, and all my tattoos were visible, apparently. I didn't realize he could see any of them. He commented that he could see ALL of them and planned on getting to know them very well. Although it was a sweet thing to say, it was a departure from how he had previously spoken to me. So, it freaked me the hell out.

Later, he asked me why I suddenly got up and left with little to no explanation—a reasonable question since we had been having a nice time. Poor guy didn't know that I always needed to be one step ahead of that sneak-attack-kiss.

It took us weeks to have our first kiss, maybe a month or more. He didn't know that I would never make the first move, which was complicated by the fact that I had never met a man who never made the first move before. Although I was grateful for it, he was the first guy I ever met that missed the sneak-attack-kiss memo. He told me he had always been in relationships with women who were the aggressors and made all the moves. Surprise(!), I wanted to tell him that he would die before I ever made the first move. The long awaited first kiss finally happened one night in my living room as he was leaving. He had his backpack on and he took a deep breath and he kissed me. At the time it was the best kiss I ever had. He felt it too and I saw all the anxiety leave his face. He smiled at me and I felt him relax and we kept kissing. There were nights after that when all we did was kiss, for hours. It was blissful. Who was I? Why had I been so scared to kiss someone?

I didn't want to come right out and tell him that at 30 years old I was a virgin. How do you casually slide that into a conversation? He figured it out one night when we were in my kitchen making drinks and he was asking me about my past relationships. My lack of relationships spoke for itself. When he realized that I was a virgin, he said it out loud, letting his freshly made bourbon and ginger ale crash to the floor. It was dramatic, but we were both grateful to have the task of cleaning up the mess while he processed this information. It was soon after this that I asked him to get tested for STDs, which all my years at the Teen AIDS Hotline led me to believe was not only the responsible thing to do but a reasonable request. I had asked Mister Ghost to do it too. He complained mildly that he didn't like needles but later told me he was able to study while he waited at student health so it was not a total waste of time.

When he told me which STDs he got tested for, I asked if he could get tested for HIV. He sent me an email stating that he had to rewrite said email several times because he was so angry. He wanted to know exactly what I wanted him to go back to get tested for because he didn't exactly like needles. I was shocked he was so angry and also confused because I thought it was clear what I was asking him to get tested for. I felt horrible. I could also feel the anger in his email. I didn't know this angry guy. What happened to the baby voice I hated? I asked some of my friends if they asked this of their partners and although they admitted that maybe they should have, no one had. In another angry email, Mister Loner told me he went back to get tested and that he "passed the test." He even offered to send me the results. I declined.

Apparently, his baby voice was hiding some serious anger issues. This is when I started to put aside my needs so that I could do everything in my power not to trigger his anger again.

SDH secretly took a picture of us kissing on our first New Year's Eve together at my friend Thomas' house. She sent it to me the next day and I sent it to Mister Loner. He didn't post much to Facebook and I had thought he was a private person. But when I logged on the next day at work, he had posted this intimate picture of us kissing. I was shocked, gasping out a very audible, "OH MY GOD." I never thought I would be the subject of a public, romantic declaration. To this point, my life had not followed the stereotypical rom-com plot.

It's always exciting for me when one of my good friends meets a new love interest. I want to know everything they know about them so we can go on this journey together, and my friends are no different from me. Thomas picked me up one night and, for some reason, it was time to show him just how close Mister Loner lived to me. On our way to dinner, we took a detour by his apartment. I have no idea why, but when I pointed out his apartment complex, Thomas rolled down his window and started screaming BOLO, a la Marlon Brando in *A Streetcar Named Desire*, into the night. To this day, I wonder if Mister Loner heard him.

In this brief time of bliss with Mister Loner, I changed my ringtone to "Wouldn't it be Nice" by the Beach Boys. It didn't last long because it corrupted my phone. I should have taken that as an omen.

There was a night when he came over extremely upset. I saw a side of him I had never seen before. He was angry and I was confused as to why his anger was directed at me. There was no sign of his annoying baby voice. He wasn't screaming, but every word hit me with nothing but anger. What in the world did I do?

He accused me of being in a bubble. I agreed and had to explain to him that it was a bubble of my own making and that I was letting him in my bubble. This only made him angrier. He sat at my dining room table demanding answers. Why were we always doing things I wanted to do and watching shows I wanted to watch? And why were we only hanging out one day a week. He said that he was used to women wanting him around all the time and that he felt responsible for entertaining them. I asked if these women were normally younger than him, and he said, yes. I told him that I would always share with him what I was up to and that he had the freedom to join or not. He was like, but what if I want to spend every night with you? My mouth opened; I was shocked. He had this look on his face like, you finally understand, you, Mary, are the problem.

No potential romantic partner had ever wanted that before: more of me. I thought I was doing him and our relationship a favor by limiting our time together as well as my demands from him. I asked if he was breaking up with me because it wasn't clear. He was angry at me but asked to spend more time with me.

The thing was, he had time and no other friends. What happened to those guys I had met at OCSC during our second date? I never saw them again. He wasn't performing his music anymore. He wasn't skateboarding anymore. I asked him when he was competing in skateboarding competitions, how he would place—I was curious. "First, I was always first."

I don't have a lot of regrets but I regret not being able to see him skateboard. One day we were in my garage and I forgot my sister Katie had asked me to hold onto a longboard she had left over from our time living at the beach in South Carolina. When he saw it, his whole body froze. He thought about it for a few minutes and then quickly told me just to, "Please, put it away." I kept it out of sight from that day forward. I can't imagine what it took for him to not get on the board. He was still working on his music, so I wanted to encourage that. I asked him what he needed and he told me about some drum software, but it was too expensive. I found what I thought he needed on eBay and won the auction, but then it turned out not to be compatible with his laptop. He had to send it back. I didn't try again to help.

Mister Loner hadn't been breaking up with me at all, he just needed time to "heal", apparently. I vowed to "change". I felt like I was losing him and I didn't have a clear reason why.

This felt like a problem I needed to solve at the moment or risk losing him. In school when I took tests, I received extra time because of my learning disability. Now, with no extra time (and no support from the public school system), I was not only unable to solve the problem, I made it worse. I thought by eliminating any type of pressure on our relationship, it would make him want to be in it more. I will never forget his face when I told him, "I don't need you for anything. You are in my life only because I want you in my life." I thought a man would love to hear that! It would be so freeing and he would be grateful. He sat in silence for a while, then said, "No one has ever said something like that to me." Still clueless and thinking this was helping, I went further to make sure he understood just how much I didn't need him. I explained that he need not worry! When I encounter a tough problem or get caught in a jam, he was not only not at the top of the list of people to call, he wasn't even on my list. What a gift!

He had no words. I wasn't angry. It was just the truth.

In retrospect, it was something I should have left unsaid. Little did I know this relationship-changing meltdown would be the first of three major meltdowns before we broke up. There were also several more after that.

In my journal from that time, there is a page titled, "The Third and Final Meltdown." The entry is completely blank except for the date. His anger was something I went to great lengths to avoid, if I could. Relationship PTSD is real. I still find myself doing this *deferring-to-the-man* thing with Mister Manicorn and he will look me in the eyes and tell me to stop. Mister Loner never told me to stop and it took me a while to realize this was how he would end up ensuring that I would hang on a few years after he broke up with me.

Mister Loner gave me a CD of his music. I was not surprised that it was soft, beautiful, and incredibly sad. It just said BOLO across the small, shiny circle.

Later he showed me lyrics to a song he was working on. I wish I had never read them. He was writing about a woman who other women could not compete with. Obviously, the woman in question wasn't me, so why would he share that as he was rubbing my leg? Touching me or not, it was just hurtful. Directly across from his bed in his bedroom, hung a portrait of a blond, pixie-like woman. It was the only picture in his room. I never had the courage to ask who she was, so I made her the image of his ex-girlfriend in my mind. She was too pretty and I didn't want her to be real. I was beginning to resent his ex-girlfriend. To me, she had become the prototypical manic pixie dream girl and there are few things I hate more than a manic pixie dream girl showing up to save the male lead from himself.

Then a pixie-sized bomb dropped. One Thursday night in my kitchen, while we were making dinner and Mister Loner was washing his hands, I asked how his day went and he just said that he had finally gotten the ring back. This was progress for him but a major hiccup for me. I had no idea he had proposed to his last girlfriend. She had accepted the ring, said she would think about marrying him, and then she kept the ring. What kind of girl keeps the ring after saying she will think about it? She later shared with him that she had unsuccessfully tried to pawn it. How did he not know that you can't marry the manic pixie dream girl?

Mister Loner was asking me what he should do with the ring now: keep or sell? Keep it for what? Me? Certainly not. I am not ring-worthy. Even if by some mistake it was offered to me, it is a hand-me-down ring steeped in bad luck. I could never wear it.

My mind was reeling. I had no idea he was capable of all of this. It seemed so out of character for what I knew about him. Now all I could hear was the Beach Boys singing in my head, "Help Me Rhonda." I have never answered to the name Rhonda, but suddenly I felt like I should. Was I Rhonda? Is that what he was secretly calling me behind my back? Was I being used to get this other woman out of his heart? I was so confused. I didn't think he wanted to get married. I had already decided that he was not capable of giving me my Simple Kind of Life vis-à-vis Gwen Stefani.

Later, I learned that things had not been going well with his last girlfriend, which is why and when he had proposed to her. It was an extreme, last-ditch gesture he made to keep her. I felt less like Rhonda, but still I was confused. We never discussed the ring again and I never saw it.

I did, however, get a rubber band from him. He always had a rubber band on his wrist. I had jokingly asked him if it was a fashion statement, but he said it was a byproduct of his work. He always ended up with a rubber band on his wrist when he left his job as a "pencil pusher" (his words) at the UNC Kenan-Flagler Business School. One day at breakfast, he had on two rubber bands. I asked what that meant and if he'd had a particularly bad day at work. Without skipping a beat or saying a word, he took one off and put it on my wrist. I wore it every day until we broke up.

While visiting my sister Katie in California, I got a tattoo of an anatomically correct heart with a syringe lying underneath. The heart has a cross stitch pattern that I saw in *BUST* magazine and the tattoo looks cross stitched into my back. The tattoo artist who inked the tattoo initially told me she was booked. It is impossible for me to hide my emotions on my face. Whatever she saw in my visage after she told me she was booked, prompted her to ask me what I wanted to get anyway. When I showed her the image I had torn out of *BUST*, she simply said, "Dope. Come back tomorrow."

That led to us being in the tattoo shop alone and her apologizing when the phone rang. She said it was her MVP and had to answer. It was an older man who told her he was dying but he came in every week for a different owl tattoo. She didn't know what it all meant but there he was every week with a different owl image. She asked me if I would still be getting tattoos when I was an old lady. I didn't think I would be, but now looking back, and 40 plus tattoos later, I could very well be someone's old lady MVP client getting cross stitch tattoos instead of sitting around doing the real thing. The tattoo was for Mister Loner, and it was meant to illustrate that he injected life into my heart.

Mister Loner and I went out for almost a year. Remember when I told you about "Dip into Art," when he didn't move from his position in the kitchen next to the punch bowl and a vodka bottle, for the entire night? I knew he wasn't doing well but I didn't know how to help him. At one point, I could see that Curtis had made his way over to his corner to talk to him for a while and in Curtis' presence, like most people, he seemed calm, talkative, and I think I even saw him laugh. I really need Curtis to create his own line of conversation cards.

Mister Loner had really tried. I know he did. He said he could not pretend to be something he wasn't. Instead of staying over and helping me clean up, like he had promised earlier, he rode off into the night on his bike. The next day he came over and broke up with me in person. I knew it was over the moment I realized his wrists were bare. In addition to him wearing rubber bands, I had purchased us a pack of Silly Bandz in the shape of musical instruments and we had split the pack and each wore them every day. It always comforted me to see that we were wearing the same wrist accessories, but as soon as he sat down, I commented that they were missing and instantly started to cry. I was heartbroken. He said that I deserved better and that he was too depressed. I received a text the next morning asking if I still wanted to be together. Huh? Of course, I wanted to still be together, I had still not learned to take a hint.

I told him I did not want to break up, but I had posted about our breakup on Facebook and he used that against me, as a reason he didn't want to get back together with me. He told me he was a private person. I think he just read the comments and didn't like what he read.

The comments weren't disparaging of him, they were just random friends and family showing me love. It took years for me to ask him why he even went on Clash in the first place. "I thought I could do it," he said. I asked this out of frustration because I loved him. We stayed broken up, but ended up spending more time together after the break up than we had when we were together. We were like the movie *50 First Dates*. It seemed like we'd been on at least that many dates and then some. Initially, when attempting to explain this new relationship status to my friends, I referred to Mister Loner as the brain-damaged Drew Barrymore character. But, turns out, that was me. I kept expecting more, that we would get back together and go back to normal dating. But he was only capable of so much, especially if he was to remain the loner, he told me he was.

I had puked twice with Mister Loner. The first time he held my hand on my vintage, yellow pleather couch and told me he had feelings for me. I puked right then and there and stayed in the bathroom for hours. He fell asleep on the yellow couch. When I could finally emerge from the bathroom, I joined him on the couch. He kept asking me what happened and all I could say was, "I just don't know." The second time was one summer at the beach.

After we broke up, we would go to the beach for a week every summer. This was when I had the hardest time with our relationship and the fact that we were not "officially" together. It felt like we were together because we lived together and spent every second together on these beach vacations. So, for a week, I was living my romantic, seaside dream/delusion.

We would be on the beach all day and then cook seafood-vacay dinners in the evenings. When alternating between reading and napping in my beach chair, he'd make sure I had an umbrella that completely shaded my "bar skin." I wasn't familiar with the term bar skin until my dermatologist told me that I had it. "I never heard of that before, is it a clinical term?" I asked with panic in my voice. He told me that due to my heritage (Irish) I had skin that was meant to be in a bar and not the sun. If I am not covered in sunscreen, I will get burned while briefly dining al fresco or driving with the car window rolled down and my arm resting in the window frame. I

111

curse my bar skin. It makes me think of something my friend Mike once said: "Everything is genetic. Being a man is genetic. That's my excuse!"

I didn't know Mister Loner had been moving my beach umbrella while I slept, following the arc of the sun in the sky. Then, while he was in the ocean and I was reading, a lady came up to me with a huge smile on her face. "He is Sooo sweet!" she said, filling me in on his caring, thoughtful movements.

On one of these beach vacations, we had even slipped up and slept together. During another, he told me he loved me. It was only the second time he had said it and it was roughly a year from the first. It was such a rare moment that I had written them both down. The first time he said I love you was after we broke up and we were in my kitchen and he looked right into my eyes and said it. All I felt was extreme sadness. I had wanted to hear it for so long, but we were not together, so why say it? It felt like he was saying it only to hurt me. I felt like I loved him so much more than he could ever love me. I also felt he knew that. Good times.

We were at the beach the second time he said it. I puked everywhere. It was just too much. He cleaned it up using a whole roll of paper towels as I washed myself up and headed to bed alone. Cleaning up puke without being asked, that is love.

So even though we had officially broken up, we continued to talk and hang out, almost constantly. In addition to the lunches, dinners, movies, hangouts, and beach vacations, we had a standing bird watching date on Saturday mornings. This is something that HE loved. On the rare occasion I could actually find a bird in my binoculars, I had no idea what bird I was looking at.

He bought me my own binoculars, so I really tried. He would pick me up and bring me coffee and then we would share lunch after. I knew he didn't have a lot of money, so it made it even more special that he would buy our lunch at Weaver Street. I could tell he thoughtfully picked out a sandwich and side salad for us to share, plus beverages. I would wake up early on Saturday mornings to meet him for a hike in a botanical garden, to sit in a canoe, or to stand next to him while watching for birds in the rain, sometimes in the snow, and also on beautiful, sunny, perfect days. He was the most excited when we saw hawks, so I got two hawks tattooed on my shoulder. They're supposed to be us. I was willing to pretend I enjoyed birding just so we had all this time together. Even though we had broken up, I had fallen more in love with him on the flip side or, more accurately, the "B-side," for BOLO.

Of course, we still exchanged Christmas presents after breaking up. One year, he left a present at my door. He texted me to tell me he had dropped it off. It became the only present under my tree because I was going to wait until he was there to open it. I would sit there and stare at it for hours. I was on the phone with my friend Evelyn one night and I told her about it. And without skipping a beat, she asked me if the package was ticking. I laughed and she dismissed my laughter, saying, "Seriously, do Sophie and Lucy bark at it?"

My friend Thomas came over and spoke directly to the present. He thought that Mister Loner was using it to spy on me and it contained some type of listening device.

It was a Pillow Pet. He had gotten me the same present he had gotten his niece and nephew. As with all of the stuffed animals that made their way into my house, my cocker spaniels thought it was for them. They became attached to this square shaped brown bear, so it eventually became their pillow pet.

There was an afternoon when we went to Mellow Mushroom on Franklin Street after looking at birds. The lights were accidentally left on in his truck, so when we went to go home, the truck wouldn't start. Mister Loner did not have anyone to call. He sighed and looked at me and said, "I guess we are walking home." I started to walk home with him and then I realized, wait, I have people to call. I called SDH and she came to our rescue in record time, like a superhero, and jumped Mister Loner's truck and then went on her way. This is the day DH earned her S and became S(uper)DH.

I had returned to the online dating scene and Mister Loner knew that. After every date fail, he was there, ready to hang out. He resented me for going on these dates and yet he didn't want to be in a relationship with me. There is a Palma Violets song called "Best of Friends," and I was living this song and listening to it often at full volume. In the end, it was he who wanted the friendship, but I wanted more. There it was, a black fly in my Chardonnay.

Three years later, I was still wanting more and realized, while on one of our beach vacays, that not only was it not going to happen, but waiting for it to happen was affecting my entire well-being. I had asked his permission, even though we were not dating, to go as Mister Ring of Fire's date to his cousin's wedding in New York. It was the weekend before our beach trip and I would miss two days at the beach. At the time, he said I didn't need to ask his permission, but I knew I did. When I got to the beach, I could sense he was already mad at me. As the week progressed, we had gotten back into our vacation groove and things were going well. It felt like we were a couple again: making dinner together and eating together as we sat on the couch watching a movie, Star Wars: Episode 1, The Phantom Menace. I was not into the annoying Jar Jar Binks character, so my head made its way to his lap–I was making moves towards us having sex! Then suddenly he was angry. He got upset about me going to be with Mister Ring of Fire. He brought up that I was out there, going on dates with people he didn't know, and he was upset at what I was possibly initiating. He went to his room and shut the door. I thought we had been clear about the reason I was dating: He didn't want to date me. I was so hurt and humiliated. I just wanted to talk. I opened his bedroom door without knocking. This brought him to a level of anger that I had never seen before. He was screaming at me, that I was just like everyone else.

I know I was wrong for opening the door, but I was desperate to resolve this and take all the blame and apologize, so we could enjoy the rest of our time at the beach. It was seeing him look at me and talk to me with such anger that finally snapped me out of it. This was not healthy. I would rather be alone than feel that way.

I closed his door. I packed up all my stuff, and at 7am, without a word, I fled the beach. Living up to my nickname, Produx, it took me several trips to the car to load it up. I was being quiet, but I know he must have heard me. He didn't emerge until I was backing out of the driveway. He had parted the curtains and was watching me from above.

That was our last beach trip and my last image of him. Then he started calling me. The first two times I didn't pick up. When I realized he would not stop calling, I picked up and his voice went from the soft baby voice, to crying, to urgent and angry. I was not turning around. The only way I got him to stop calling was to give in and to promise to talk to him later. We would meet.

My next conversation was with my father who was watching my cocker spaniels while I was away. I called to tell him I was coming home early and that I would be there to pick up the dogs in a couple hours. My father asked why I was coming home, and I just responded that I needed to "flee the beach."

"I have no idea what that means nor do I want to, but I will have coffee waiting for you when you arrive," he said. That was all I needed.

I texted Mister Ring of Fire when I got back to my parent's house and his first response was, "That baby really is an asshole." He had recently told me his favorite line from *Sex and the City* came out of Samantha's mouth, "Babies are not my scene. From what I've heard, this one sounds like an asshole." It was so accurate. He asked if I was OK and I told him I had stopped by Sunrise Biscuit Kitchen to get a fried chicken biscuit to go with my dad's coffee. Everything was perfect.

I am lucky I have friends and family who save me from myself. I don't share this with everyone, in the event that it could be used against me, but I cannot go back on a pinky swear. It is something cemented in my head from childhood. When our pinkies lock, it is a legally binding agreement. The night that I fled the beach, I was at the secret bar in Carrboro with SDH discussing what happened over some very potent Manhattans and all of a sudden she looked me in the eye, stuck out her pinky, and said promise me you will never contact him again. SDH had come to my rescue again. I promised her, we pinky swore, and I never made contact again.

JK.

You know it is never that easy.

These are the last text messages I sent to Mister Loner. First, I should tell you that Mister Loner would text me words of affection that he would never say to me in person. One was "amo" and the other was "babers." Both, perhaps, were remnants of past relationships. I never asked.

25 May 2013 1:35 PM: Me: "I think it is time we part ways for good. I obviously can't handle this relationship with you. I will miss you.

25 May 2013 5:51 PM: Mister Loner: Donger. I am sorry i didn't show you how much you meant to me. I will miss you too."

12 Jun 2013 10:01 PM: Mister Loner: "I hope you are happier with no b. That is what I got from your email. So, I will miss you. But respect your wishes. Amo.

15 Jun 2013 11:34 PM: Me: Amo!!!!

16 Jun 2013 9:27 PM: Me: I was at OCSC last night so I was thinking of you. I do miss you.

23 Jun 2013 10:29 AM: Mister Loner: I like getting your texts. You have to tell me if I am supposed to respond.

24 Jun 2013 9:59 PM: Mister Loner: I was not being a smart ass. I honestly don't know anymore. I only know i got kicked out of your circle. amo anyway

10 Jul 2013 11:51 PM: Me: I miss you!!!!

11 Jul 2013 7:13 PM: Mister Loner: I miss you too. You have the power.

This is when the power of my pinky swear to SDH kicked in. It is also when I started listening to Lucinda Williams' song "Changed the Locks". I listened to it loud while I screamed all the words and was always left feeling empowered even if it made me cry. I saw her sing it live once, before I knew Mister Loner, and it gave me the chills, but I didn't understand her desperation until now. When Lucinda sang the song, she was so beautiful in her wrinkly t-shirt, unbrushed hair, and smeared eye makeup. She roared the words. I needed to change the kind of car I drove, the kind of clothes I wore, and perhaps even the number on my phone, too. I never did change my number, but it wasn't until I changed my clothes, car, hair, and the town I lived in, that I felt totally free of Mister Loner.

Nine

Mister Portugal

Carrboro/Chapel Hill, NC circa 2010

My first date back on Clash.com was for brunch at my regular place with Mister Portugal. I had hope that my second tango with the Clash algorithm would not result in a series of spectacular disappointments. I agreed to go out with Mister Portugal because he seemed to be the opposite of Mister Loner. In one of Mister Portugal's profile pictures, he was dressed in a generic polo shirt and jeans, sitting in an office chair, looking directly at me through a lightly glowing screen. I found this refreshing because it looked like he wasn't trying to be anything other than exactly himself. He seemed safe.

I then read that he was Portuguese and that sealed the deal. My sister Katie is married to a man, Justin, a man who is half Portuguese and nothing short of wonderful, so I was encouraged by the fact that he was 100 percent Portuguese. Justin is dedicated to his craft. When he's not cooking, he's watching food documentaries, reading cookbooks, and, from what I have seen, he's always learning new things that make him a better chef. He is my sister's equal in terms of drive and anger (Katie told me that Justin might be angrier than her, which I find hard to believe), and they are both funny, although my father will point out, like it is an indisputable fact, that Katie is funnier than Justin. They taught a cooking class together and of course the entire family was there and they were both hilarious and charming. Our father was visibly proud. Dad has always cared far more about whether his daughters are smart and interesting than how they look. He comments that his girls are beautiful but has never criticized our appearances. He left that to our mother. Anyway, it's weird for me to comment on my brother-in-law at all. My sisters and I have an unspoken rule that we do not discuss our relationships. We never have, and when I have tried in the past, just to see if we are capable of having this type of conversation, it never goes well. Katie has literally fought with other women over Justin, but that was a long time ago. She has stopped talking to me mid-sentence as she smiles and watches him walking towards us. I commented on this one day and she got embarrassed, flashed her dimples, and said, "Well, he is my husband."

Mister Portugal is deaf in his left ear, which I learned at the beginning of the date by accident. After we placed our drink order, I had leaned in to tell him that we—my friends Crafty and SDH, with whom I brunch nearly every Sunday at this very spot—always get the same sweet, well-meaning but gets-everything-wrong waitress. He only responded that he was glad I leaned in and spoke in his good ear. Good ear? It was dumb luck! I had a 50/50 chance. He told me that he was from Boston and in "hard money banking" with his best friend. It was just the two of them and they had moved to North Carolina together, but they had a lot of business back in Boston. The more he alluded to his career as a hard money banker, the more confused I became. Then he mentioned, almost in passing, that he owns a school in Florida for kids with special needs. I had no idea what to make of that. I couldn't ask any follow-up questions because he was constantly talking. When I started to talk, he would just talk over me. ANNOYING. I figured I would do some research about hard money banking on my own. That way, the next time we met, I could have a more intelligent conversation with him about his job.

At the end of the date, he told me he wanted to see the documentary *Waiting for Superman* for our next date. I'd heard of the documentary, so I knew it was about the public school system, but hadn't seen it, so I agreed it would be a perfect second date activity. What luck! I had actually wanted to see this documentary, plus it would be nice to hear him *not* talk for 111 minutes. I was more excited to see this documentary than to see him again.

When Crafty, SDH, and I had signed up for this online dating adventure, we had set some ground rules. One was that every guy would get at least three dates, which is why I had agreed to see Mister Portugal again. As our dating adventures (errr curiosities) wore on, we would end up throwing every rule we made out the window. Our dates slowly became get-through-it-by-any-means-necessary scenarios. Sunday brunch was our time to discuss, learn from and support one another, heal, and most importantly, laugh.

When I got home and Googled "hard money banking", there was nothing that came up describing it as a real job. However, hard money banks themselves did come up in the search. These banks don't have names, just phone numbers, if you can find them. There wasn't even a Wikipedia page for them, which made me question their existence. I was in uncharted territory! After a mental shrug, I decided that I would have to ask him directly and brace myself for the inevitable, long, and involved response.

Unfortunately, the documentary wasn't playing yet, so we decided on dinner at a local restaurant, Lantern, and then a show at the Local 506 for our second date. Mister Portugal had proposed the show at the Local 506 and I wondered at the time why he was so specific about seeing this particular show.

At Lantern, we decided to sit at the bar while we waited for our table. He told me not to freak out, but he had memorized my online dating profile. He states that he knows I like to drink. This will be one of the many times he freaks me out by referring to my profile. After his remark about my drinking, I order a dirty martini, look him in the eye and calmly state that yes, I drink, and martinis are what I like to drink the most. As I investigated his eyes, I could tell that he wanted to tell me that he already knew that. As soon as it arrived, I took a sip of my martini and wondered if he had just proposed the

Local 506 show because my profile stated that I liked live local music. It seemed likely, since he had taken the time to memorize my profile. I thought it was nice he was trying to make sure I had a good time.

Perched atop bar stools, he sat way too close to me, making sure that at least two of his limbs were always touching me. All evidence to the contrary, he verbally checks in several times and states that he is not a touchy person. I wonder if he thinks that if he says it out loud, then all the touching is okay? It is not OK. I am actually not a touchy-feely person, so I shifted around a lot and drank the martini fast. I was uncomfortable. I looked him in the eyes again and imagined him thinking, "Yup, I know her so well, she likes to drink those martinis ..."

I was still in the dark regarding the hard money banking, so I asked him to explain exactly what he did for work, which kept him talking for the next half hour. He used the phrase, "I know it sounds shady," at least half a dozen times. "Not exactly," he said when I asked him if he worked for a company. "It's more like people from the neighborhood know and trust me, so they ask for money when they need it. I give them the money and I just ask that they pay me back in six months, you know, a reasonable amount of time."

He mentioned that he's involved in a plethora of lawsuits. I kept asking questions. All I knew was that this was not a job anyone I knew had. He said he was like Rumpelstiltskin and that when the six months were up, he wanted "his baby." This is the phrase that made me see him differently. I began to mentally go through all the ways people "get their baby" from the movies. Yikes. This guy was not safe at all.

When people can't pay, does Rocky Balboa show up? Is he his own Rocky? Maybe his best friend has the Rocky job? He didn't look like he could be his own Rocky, but he didn't look like what the movies told me a loan shark looked like either, and I had picked this guy based solely on how "safe" he looked. What is wrong with me? Wait, maybe he was safe? Maybe loan sharks just get a bad rap and I assumed he wasn't safe because of his job? Plus, in every movie, the loan shark is relegated to the bad guy pile. Unfair? Maybe I watch too many movies?

I desperately wanted another martini, but I needed to stop drinking because this guy suddenly seemed like the most dangerous person I had ever met. I remembered to ask about the school he owns because that didn't seem to fit.

"Well, it isn't exactly out of the goodness of my heart." He explained that he was seeing "this crazy woman," and that the school she worked for was in financial trouble. I hate when guys use the word "crazy" to describe women. It literally explains nothing and yet the man seems to think it says everything I need to know about her. What a relief you managed to get away from yet another crazy female! How did you do it?!

Anyway, he bailed out the school and the school has not been able to pay him back. It's just that simple. Thinking back to that documentary ... Did he think he was Superman?! I wanted to tell him that this all sounded incredibly shady and the more he explained, the worse it sounded. Please shut up and ask me what my favorite color is. Please?

Since he never asked, I will share with you that my favorite color is sparkle. Yes, I have been told that sparkle is not a color and that it is a stupid answer, but it is the truth. If it has sparkles, that is the one I want. Always.

After dinner, we headed across the street to the Local 506 and sat at the bar. I ordered a sugar free red bull and pulled out my conversation cards. Normally, these cards are reserved for guys who don't want to talk, but in this case, I wanted to use them so I could talk. He insisted that we go through every single card, which he prefaced with, "All the PG ones, that is."

He became so obsessed with the cards that he forgot that they were meant for both people to answer. I could see that my plan was backfiring. In the meantime, the band had started to play and we were the only ones left at the bar.

When I finally had a chance to get an answer in, my only recourse was to yell my personal responses into his not out-of-order ear. I had totally forgotten which ear I was supposed to be talking to. The cards have some simple questions like "Are you a Brady Bunch or Partridge Family person? Explain." But, I was answering a more complex question about who I admire the most and why. The bartender kept glancing over, and he was no doubt trying to figure out what was going on and why on earth our cards had giant hearts on them. Mister Portugal shuffled through the deck three times to make sure we had gotten to all the PG cards. We had completely missed the show. When I asked why he'd wanted to go to the show in the first place, he said he drives his neighbor to work every day and she listens to this band. She was probably even there. What kind of relationship did he have with his neighbor? I was afraid to ask and it really didn't matter. In my best Joe Pesci a la *My Cousin Vinny*, "I'm finished with this guy."

My memory of Rumpelstiltskin was a little rusty, so it took me a minute to realize that, in the end, he never got his baby. He talked too much and gave himself away.

Mister Portugal held my hand as we walked to my car. As I've said before and will say many times again, I do not like unsolicited touching. To me, holding hands symbolizes togetherness or couplehood, and all I wanted to do was run from this guy. To make matters even more uncomfortable, he decided to take this time to ask me why my profile had changed. He said that he recently noticed that I changed my stance on having children and he was happy to see that. Little did he know I had disingenuously made that change because of a hunch that wanting kids would deepen the quality of my dating pool. He wanted kids. As if right on cue for this painfully quiet moment, as I uncomfortably held hands with a Loan Shark from Boston, a woman passed by, looked at me and said, "You're beautiful." Then she kept walking. It was as if he had paid for this to happen. He yelled back, "She is, isn't she!"

I need to explain that previous to this one time, no one had ever remarked, out loud, in front of me, about my looks. I don't inspire that type of remark. I go out of my way to have eccentric hair, purses, shoes, and clothes so that people don't see my actual body.

Quick story: I had a good friend, Mister Tung. We had worked together, and after we both graduated from pharmacy school, he moved to Oakland, California. During one visit, over a meal of dumplings and US Weekly (because he doesn't like to talk when eating), I remarked about how skinny some of the people in the magazine were. "No man finds your weight attractive," he responded.

I'm not sure if it was the look on my face or if he had not thought about what he said until it left his mouth, but he quickly followed with, "But I think you are perfect".

It was too late. That statement scarred me. I'm not sure if he was trying to do some brainwashing, reprogramming shit, like he would be the only one to think I was perfect, so I should just be with him? I was finished with Mister Tung too. US Weekly was better company anyway. But maybe because I was young and inexperienced, I felt like I needed to be polite and reciprocate his hospitality. So, I invited him to stay with me in Charleston for the exact number of days I had stayed with him. I didn't think he would take me up on it, but he did. I didn't even take time off from work when he came to visit. We spent a week together, eating leftovers, tutoring one of my friends and pharmacy interns in pharmacokinetics, and walking the dogs. He was just there living in my everyday life. I took him to get two tattoos he wanted and then he left without saying goodbye. We never spoke again. I used to get birthday and valentines' day cards from him, but those have stopped. The most we ever did, intimately, was hug, and that was torture. They always seemed way too long. I was not capable of being with a man who claimed he loved me when I didn't love him. Turns out, I cared more about myself than I thought I did. I think that surprised both me and Mister Tung.

My mother likes to point out that I have a "generic Irish face." Her father's side is from Ireland and I don't know exactly what that dig means, but it's not a compliment. If anyone is going to offer up a remark about me as they're passing by, it's usually to ask what perfume I'm wearing. I always wanted to be heavily perfumed, and once I could afford to, that is how I have remained. I used to go to Sephora, when I could not afford fancy perfumes, and spray on as many as I could. I have stopped doing that, but if I am reading a magazine, I will tear open all the perfume ads and rub them on my wrists. All of them. The problem is the perfumes I like always have these terrible names. When people ask a grown woman what they're wearing, the elegant answer is never Princess, Alien, Angel, or Romance.

Anyway, point being, I could not shake Mister Portugal's hand off and get to my car fast enough. He texted me after the date at 1:25 AM: "Talking with u is relaxing, thank u for a great night...I feel like I made u a little uncomfortable holding your hand, if so, apologize (im not pushy like that, just how I felt) hope i can see u again and you got home safe."

I texted back at 1:29 AM: "Glad you are home safe. Yes, I just wasn't ready for the handholding. Sorry. I hope you sleep well."

He texted me back the next day at 3:30 PM: "Hey, tomorrow is going to be another great afternoon, ive been wanting to go to the driving range and hit some balls for a little bit... I don't know if that's fun for u, probably not best in boots but its relaxing if you are interested, there would be No hand holding! And you can pay ... it's the best i can do. b"

I took some time to think about this but ended up replying at 4:56 PM: "You are a great guy but I am not the girl for you. Thank you for everything! I wish you good luck."

He responded at 5:35 PM: "Ya been getting that a lot." Then, in a separate follow up text he says: "Didnt mean that in a nasty way, ur special u deserve what you want. Take care." The final text is from me at 5:45 PM:- "Thank you. You are special too. You will find your girl. Remember, everything is perfect." This will be the first time I break the three-date rule, but it certainly will not be the last. I still think he paid that lady to yell a compliment at me and I will always cherish that manufactured moment we shared.

My cubicle mate Allyson enthusiastically texts me early the next morning to check in and ask how my date went with Mister Portugal. "So, he was all up in my grill for most of the date and then he held my hand to the car. He is out! Next up is Mister Wizard. I love you too dude. Thanks for asking. Hope you have a great weekend!!" My cubicle mate was a "hugger" who was forced to share close quarters with me and she knew the hand holding was an offense as great as the sneak-attack-kiss or a simple hug. If you really cared about me, you wouldn't touch me.

Ten

Mister Wizard

Cary, NC Circa 2010

Mister Wizard and I had brunch the morning after my last date with Mister Portugal. He told me to meet him at a restaurant in downtown Cary—the old, I mean, historic part of Cary that I hadn't even known existed. I had the realization that when I told a guy that I would meet him anywhere, that usually meant that I would come to them.

I lived a solid 30 minutes away and was exhausted from the night before, but still I got dressed in my uniform: dress, black cowboy boots, and hair all twisted up and held in place with multi-colored bobby pins. It is a variation of the hairdo that my Aunt Polly has worn for as long as I have known her. Her perfectly white hair is perpetually twisted up and held in place with a single silver barrette. I adopted this hairdo because it keeps my hair out of my face and I don't have to worry about it becoming wavy again if I have it straightened, or flat again if I have curled it. Clips and ponytail holders are just not as effective as multi-colored bobby pins.

Using this method, I can twist my hair up and cover it in hairspray and not have to worry about it until the next morning. I have often slept pins-in because the last thing you want to do at the end of the day is remove 50 pins from your head. The only downside to this regime is that it does not travel well. It sets off metal detectors and then you have to go through an awkward head pat-down, which means that a female stranger aggressively touches your head. It feels like a violation, but it is also strangely intimate. It's hard to know where to look when you're face to face with a TSA worker who is clawing your head to save lives. She was just doing her job. And in the end, the whole hairdo has to be redone—major time-suck for all involved.

For the below-neck portion of the uniform, I wore the same six dresses repeatedly. The morning of the Mister Wizard date, I had on the wannabe Versace-patterned, blue-and-gold, short-sleeved dress that was too short. I didn't think it was too short, but the office secretary had decided to share, "Brave to wear a dress that short to work." As a result of her comment, I started wearing black leggings with it—and all the dresses. Ultimately, I felt better covering my blindingly white legs, which, I figured, must have offended her.

The dress had this extra fabric part in the middle that I felt hid my stomach. With the other dresses, I would have to throw a belt on to hide my stomach, but this dress was the rare one I wore belt-freeeeee.

I am a huge fan of Tim Gunn and he taught me that "a belt can work magic". I like how Gunn has a scientific approach to fashion. I own his book, *A Guide to Quality, Taste, and Style,* in hardback. I treat it like my old pharmacy school text books: It is there for reference and I can never part with it. These dresses, leggings, belts, and boots had become my uniform because I didn't have to iron any of it, or even think about date attire at all, or worry that I would be uncomfortable—the dates seemed to provide plenty of that on their own and I didn't need to bring extra. The uniform could take me anywhere, whether or not it was appropriate, and I began to wear it every day—beach, work, dinner, parties, hiking, and even one time on a boat.

A multi-strand, multicolored, faux pearl necklace always completed the look. It is not something I would have ever picked out for myself, but while shopping with my friend Peter in a Fossil shop in

Spain, he suggested I put down the skull I wanted and purchase this necklace. The pearls are held together with this small rope that, through the years, has absorbed all my perfume. In addition to it making me feel like Peter is with me, instead of tucked away in southern Spain, the scent of the necklace brings me comfort.

One time, during a weekend getaway, I was forced to go jet skiing in-uniform. I hadn't known this was going to be an activity. I might have looked overdressed out there on the water in pearls, but I was comfortable, and my hair didn't budge.

Within moments of sitting down with Mister Wizard, I learned of his ex-wife and their two kids. Then, while he was looking up worriedly from my cowboy boots, "Just to confirm, you don't like country music, do you? My ex-wife loves it."

"No, I hate it," I replied, smiling. He elaborated on the freedom he would have after he could stop paying alimony. He had given himself the screen name Mister Wizard because he fixes machines in hospitals and according to him, he makes a lot of money. After stating several times that he really wants to tell me how much alimony he pays but, of course, will not, he tells me how much alimony he is paying his ex-wife.

While talking without taking a break, he clears his throat incessantly. I mean, it is constant, annoying, and getting in the way of our ... conversation? I started to think his ex-wife was probably out there on a date saying, "I didn't hear you clear your throat once! How refreshing!"

I broke my rule of never going to a second location, twice, with Mister Wizard. Normally, my motto is safety first, but as brunch wore on, my boredom and irritation made me want to move—and frankly, I could take him. I am 5 feet and 9 inches tall, but with these cowboy boots and hairstyle I am closer to 6 feet and no one has ever described me as delicate. Mister Wizard's favorite used-book store was close by, so we headed there.

I'm a sucker for used books, and who knew if I'd ever be there again, so I got into his car. He offered me some Ice Breakers Mints after popping two or three in his gob. I thought maybe the throat clearing would finally end.

Nope.

I practically leapt out the car when we arrived at the bookstore. A lady greeted us inside, saying they have a deal: Buy three hardcover books and your fourth is free. I'm stoked—instantaneously a woman on a mission. As we browsed, I shared with him how much I hated the book *Eat, Pray, Love*. I love a memoir, but I realized that I had fallen into the trap of reading yet another book that may have changed other women's lives but was clearly not meant for me.

I was in middle school when *The Bridges of Madison County* came out. My mother had heard that reading *The Bridges of Madison County* would change her life, but she didn't like to read, so she bought me a hardcover copy. She handed it to me and told me to read it and tell her what she needed to do to change her life. I was barely 12.

"Ew, I am not having an affair," she said, after I finished the book and told her what happened. She never spoke of the book again.

A woman from the next aisle over chimed in to our *Eat, Pray, Love* conversation. I paused and thought for sure this lady wasn't talking to us, but then Mister Wizard looked down the aisle and his eyes went huge and his face went flush as she rounded the corner and walked toward us. She was looking straight at me and not at any of the books. I smiled at her as she passed. Mister Wizard was freaking out. His red hue deepened and he appeared to be frozen.

When he finally snapped out of it, he looked around and then leaned in and started whispering. He could tell me what was going on, but he couldn't tell me in the store.

I was focused on getting my four books. I stayed blissfully unaware of how crazy the situation actually was until we got back in the car. As I browsed, Mister Wizard dawdled behind me on his phone, freaking out over some text messages. I don't think he looked at one book. I was searching for the Dale Carnegie book *How to Win Friends and Influence People*. I had heard it referred to during a *This American Life* broadcast. I thought, maybe, it would help make the 1-on-1's with my supervisor at work less painful. Perhaps it would even make me less reliant on my conversation cards! After I purchased the Dale Carnegie book, a couple Tori Spelling memoirs, and an Eckhart Tolle book that was supposed to change my life, it was time to leave and finally find out why Mister Wizard was so worked up.

Back in his car, he popped more mints, looked around, and used the word "taper" to describe the status of his last relationship. He was still hanging out with this particular woman, who I gathered was not his ex-wife, but every day it was less and less. He said it was hard because they had dated for a year and both had kids and a lot in common … I did not share this with him at the time, but "taper" is something you do with prescription steroids, not women. "Taper" implies some indiscernible degree of togetherness. The woman on the other end of his "taper" was the woman at the bookstore. She was probably at brunch too, he added casually. "She was probably stalking us all along," he said. STALKING.

"She knows I'm going out on dates with other women," he continued as my eyes turned into saucers. "Maybe it was all just a coincidence." Right. "Fuck You," the woman had texted Mister Wizard while we were in the used-book store. "She must have seen my car and wanted to cause a scene."

"Why?"

"I don't know."

I expected more insight.

He pops some more mints.

"There's a park nearby and it is a beautiful day. Should we take a walk?"

Against my better judgment, I agreed to go to location number three with Mister Wizard, and it was not because I wanted more time with him. He had me so stressed out that a walk before my journey home sounded nice.

He pointed out that we walk at the same pace; something he and his ex-wife never did. He comments on my height. "That's a relief because my ex-wife is short, so this will be better for my back in the long run." Better for his back? He was really getting carried away here. Mister Wizard hadn't asked me one question that didn't directly relate to his ex-wife. It felt like she was stalking our date too.

I was busy scanning the area for his stalker ex-girlfriend when something my sister Katie told me suddenly popped into my head.

Katie and I were born 19 months apart and we fought a lot growing up, verbally and physically. We shared a bed, wore the same clothes and shoe size, shared a bathroom ... She told me that even though I was bigger and stronger than her, she had "the rage", so she would always win when we fought. I began to fear this woman the same way I feared my sister's rage growing up. I was ready to head home.

Before checking the back seat and then getting in my car and heading back to Carrboro where I belonged, I had lied to Mister Wizard and told him I would like to do it all again. I later told him via text that I was not the girl for him. I know, it is a punk move, but what did I owe Mister Wizard? Nada. I texted my coworker Mike after the date to tell him I found a hardcopy version of *How to Win Friends and Influence People* and, get this, it was free!

Eleven

Mister Egg Beard

Greensboro, NC circa 2011

I have only had decaf once in my life and it was by accident—the opposite of a Christmas miracle. My parents were coming to visit my sister Katie and me in South Carolina, so I made a special trip to Starbucks to buy the holiday blend. I had never purchased it before and in the Starbuckian chaos, I picked up the decaffeinated version. I made the celebratory coffee when the fam arrived and everyone was enjoying the taste, and then the complaints started rolling in. Besides it not being strong enough (err, at all), the headaches were coming on, strong. I made more, of course, and stronger, with extra scoops. Still, no one was happy—the opposite. I didn't understand it! Then, a few days later when they left and I had time to examine my holiday failures, I checked to see if it had expired. As I was scanning the label, I spotted it. There it was, in tiny print, the D-word: "Decaffeinated". I felt betrayed. It was the same exact taste as full-blown coffee but the *feeling* was totally absent. What a waste of time.

I never put too much stock in Clash.com profile headlines. My profile's headline simply read, "Decaf is a waste of time." My next date started with a wink and a tagline: "Never be afraid to try something new. Remember, amateurs built the ark. Professionals built the Titanic." Maybe this is how he landed dates, by winking and then having his tagline suggest he was something new ... Or was he religious? Captain of a boat? A ship chaplain?

He is from Pennsylvania, like me. He is my same age. He has tattoos. I was sold.

After I returned the wink, we exchanged a few emails.

"It's awesome that you have tattoos," I said. "I think it's *more* awesome that you have tattoos," he offers. "I definitely dig a girl with tats." Then I suggested brunch, using the line I always regret, "I am happy to meet you anywhere." Change is hard!

The tattoo connection was encouraging since we didn't listen to the same music or watch the same movies. Considering my other online dates, I knew absolutely that no decisions should be based on his profile pictures alone. It's only when you meet eye-to-eye or eye-to-top-of-his-head, that you are faced with the truth.

At the time, my hairdresser Leslie was also online dating and we would spend our time together exchanging war stories. "If I get out of the car and see that he isn't as tall as he said he was, I get right back in my car and leave with no explanation at all," Leslie said, shears in one hand, comb in the other.

I started laughing. "You just leave without a word? Isn't that a little extreme? Why do you care that much about height?" She got angry just mulling this over. "Think about it, if they lie about their height, then they will lie about anything!"

I guess this could be true. Her anger suggested she had probably tested this theory and proven it to be true. I admired her technique. No time wasted, not even with an explanation. My new strategy was to eliminate all the back and forth and just try to meet the person as soon as possible because everything seems normal until we sit down face to face.

I wanted to get to that point quicker. In this case, because I may have rushed things too much, we both had missed one key geographic element: He lived in Greensboro—an hour's drive from Carrboro and me. We were GUDs: Geographic UnDesirables, with respect to one another. How did I miss that?! Damn small print. What a headache.

He did not realize I lived in Carrboro until I casually mentioned it at brunch. I didn't feel so bad because he missed the small print too. The hour-long drive was a reflection of how desperate I was at that point. He had the slightest bit of promise, so I had put the pedal to the metal. "You don't live in Greensboro?" he said, before quickly coming up with a solution. "If we ever move in together, we would have to move to Mebane [*meb-in*]," he said, because it was halfway between our current residences.

STOP!!

Move in together? I owned a townhouse in Carrboro that I loved. He lived in an apartment with his best friend, which he pointed out was chosen because it's within walking distance to the bars. It became clear we were both literally and figuratively in two different places.

"There's my roommate right now!" he said, pointing, as we dug into brunch. "This is the time of day he goes for a run." I watched him as he watched his roommate run for a while in silence. I feel he is longing to be with him running or just maybe longing not to be sitting there with me. Whatever it was, it was apparent the bromance between them was strong.

None of my tattoos were showing, as usual, but his full sleeve was on full display. The tattoos are mostly dedicated to his two favorite bands, the Grateful Dead and The Beatles.

STOP!!

I have never actually heard a Grateful Dead song, at least that I am aware of. I have been exposed to various songs by The Beatles because I live on planet Earth, but I have never listened to them voluntarily.

"Cool," I mustered, when he showed me his tattoos.

My mind wandered. I was still painting my nails before each date, which was really slowing me down. On a recent trip to the drug store, I saw these Sally Hansen nail stickers and I thought I would give them a whirl. They smelled like nail polish but required no drying time. Magic. They also came in all of these fun patterns, so for every date I had fresh, interesting nails. Some of the patterns were so intricate that people would ask me where I got them done. There was even one early morning flight when the TSA officer remarked "Wow!" when he saw my nails. "Did you paint them yourself?" I looked him straight in the eye, "Yes, I was up all night!" I waited a beat and then smiled. He did not smile back.

The thing about the nails is that the TSA officer was the only man to really notice and comment on them. For reasons I can't explain, I felt I needed to have my nails done for every date, but honestly, I don't think any of the guys on the dates noticed, least of all cared about my nails—they just weren't a high priority area for the male gaze on a first date.

I was also carrying around an AstroTurf purse. It is a traditional Kate Spade handbag with AstroTurf covering the entire outside, with a light-colored plaid fabric on the inside. Since it was a literal handbag, I entered every room AstroTurf first. It had one downfall; it was a nightmare at a buffet. This is how it goes: Me trying to keep the overstuffed AstroTurf in my elbow crook AND balance a plate with my hand on the same arm AND gauge what food looks like it won't hurt me. What a workout! I only made that mistake once. Anyway, it was my latest attempt at an accessory to distract from my body. The Turf purse was a conversation starter and it worked like a charm. I felt like people only saw the AstroTurf purse, not me, when I walked in a room. At my local Trader Joe's, I would hear the crew saying, "The AstroTurf is back!" This is the only purse I have ever had that elicits an equal number of comments from men and women.

"How many dogs have peed on it?" asked my ophthalmologist. Later I smelled the purse, just to be sure.

Mister Egg Beard had the Pennsylvania accent that I'm familiar with and it gave me a false sense of security. If you are not familiar with a Pennsylvania accent, the closest relative is the Baltimore accent, but instead of being called "Hon," you will probably be referred to as "Yinz" and asked if you wanted a glass of "wooder" (aka water). My favorite Pop Culture Happy Hour podcaster, Glen Weldon, said it best when he was describing the Pennsylvania-based show "Mare of Easttown."

"All these vowels! It is like crawling into a cheesesteak!"

The Pennsylvania accent is the Pennsylvania accent, and it is music to my ears. Instant comfort. In addition to missing the accent and my family, of course, in Pennsylvania, I have a constant craving for Hershey's chocolate (or as my friend Irina lovingly refers to it, "American bullshit chocolate"). I also crave Tastykakes and soft pretzels—if you know, you know. I still remember the day I was driving my dad's Pontiac Bonneville and looked in the door pocket and found a bag of mini-Hershey bars. You can take us out of Pennsylvania, but we will always love bullshit American chocolate.

Coworker Mike is also from Pennsylvania. When you take calls all day long from all over the U.S., you start to notice some trends. One we always made note of was that anyone calling from Pennsylvania was nice. We would hang up, look at each other, and say "another nice person from Pennsylvania", and then smile. Perhaps you could say we were biased, but Pennsylvania never let us down.

Mister Egg Beard is bald, but in an attempt to make up for it, he had a very full and long beard. True to his lack of effort on this date, he ordered the same breakfast as me, but he didn't get his eggs scrambled, which was a bad move on his part. As he was talking and eating, his over-easy eggs were getting all over his beard and as much as I pointed and said, "You have a little something there," he was not able to make a dent in the amount of eggs clinging to it. We were definitely not at the point where I could touch him, nor did I want to, and at a certain point I was annoying myself with my attempts to direct him to the egg. I had to let it go and move on.

The more I tried not to see the egg, the more I felt like I was in a *Seinfeld* episode and it was all I could focus on—all that egg goop and beard hair, it was gnarly. What did it smell like? What else could be in there? I was making myself nauseated. I tried to imagine kissing him.

STOP!!

I couldn't. I found myself looking into his eyes, just so I didn't look at the egg-beard again.

My mom still felt the need to remind me that according to her psychic, the guy I was searching for had blue eyes and traveled during the week. (Egg Beard's eyes were not blue). These were two extremely specific details that I was not looking for in a man. I could care less what color his eyes were, and traveling during the week did not seem ideal. This information coming from my mother's psychic was not helpful, as usual. What am I supposed to do with that non-information? What about a name? Gimme a name! First and last, preferably, and maybe an email too, please.

Initially and inexplicably, after what would be our one and only date, I did give him a rating of five Zelda hearts. We'd had a normal (enough) date. I didn't even need any of my conversation cards.

Plus, he didn't make me want to bolt. But there was no magic, no spark, and, ultimately, nothing that made me excited to see him and that egg-beard again.

This is as good of a time as any to bring up "Sex and the City" and the massive impact it had on me. I do not think of myself as lucky, but when it came to the timing of when this show was airing and how old I was, I consider myself luuucky. In Charleston, when I was living with my sister Katie and friend Monte from pharmacy school, we didn't have HBO. We'd meet on Sunday nights at a downtown movie theater to watch the latest episode. We'd down martinis, other people would dress up, and it would be a packed house every time—not just one theater, it was all of them. It was an event! Later, we would learn this was completely illegal but at the time it was the highlight of my week. We won't dwell on the Manolo's that I found at a thrift store one time (had to have, paid a small fortune for, and have worn exactly 20 minutes). "Sex and the City" made it crystal clear to me that settling was not an option. It was OK, if not glamorous, to be older and not married because, in the words of Mary J. Blige, "I'm searching for a real love." Don't settle for Baryshnikov just because he's Baryshnikov. I know these are fictional ladies in fictional relationships, but when I was watching episodes for the millionth time (with the commentary from Michael Patrick King), I felt like I was in a class.

I just wanted the real deal—true fucking love—but with someone who loved me back. Duh. I wanted it so bad because I had felt it before. The problem was, I felt it with one of my best friends who wasn't ready to come out yet, Mister Ring of Fire. I have a ring of fire tattoo which is just a plain red perfect circle on my back. When I explained the significance of the tattoo to the artist in Park City, Utah, Jack, he told me he had a ring of fire too; she had worked just a few feet away in the piercing portion of the parlor. She left him and their business, but he still loved her. He took his time with that red circle tattoo as he told me all about it. When I went back the next year, he and the shop were both gone. There are a million reasons why he could have closed down, but the first thing I thought of was that it just became too painful. He had to save himself.

I learned the history of the Johnny Cash song "Ring of Fire" from another episode of *This American Life*. June Carter wrote the song and it was originally titled "Love's Ring of Fire." She was married and Johnny Cash was married (not to her) and after touring together, she realized she loved him. But they couldn't be together, so it was painful, like falling into a ring of fire. And oh, how it burned!

I could not be with Mister Ring of Fire because he could never love me the same way I loved him, so without even meaning to, he pushed me into that ring of fire and it fucking burned! I talked endlessly about it to my friends, read a ton of books, and consumed gallons of vodka. The only thing that made me feel better was a contestant on the finale of "*A Shot at Love with Tila Tequila*."

It was down to just two contestants and they were doing the final interviews before Tila made her choice. One contestant said something so profound I think it actually healed me—in the moment I heard it anyway. This dude said even if she doesn't pick him at least he got to feel that feeling and to know that it does exist, what it feels like to be in love. I never watched the show, I was just scrolling around and this guy was speaking directly to my heart. It felt like the truth. He instantly made me feel better and reminded me of that pesky attitude of gratitude I am always forgetting about. I needed to feel grateful that I even experienced it. I was happy for him and this super healthy attitude but I also hoped this guy wasn't about to go into the ring of fire, so I turned off the TV before I could find out. I had done plenty of crying and I wasn't about to cry over *A Shot of Love with Tila Tequila* too.

Post Mister Egg Beard, I decided to read his profile more carefully, to see what else I had missed. He was, "looking for a fun-loving girl that knows how to have a good time and doesn't take herself too seriously. Someone who enjoys music, art and the outdoors is a plus. My ideal match would be someone that can be silly and have fun, but also knows when to be serious. Someone that is laid back, and always has a smile." Sure, that sounds like it could be me on a good day after a glass of wine or two.

We continued to text for two weeks, just checking-in, nothing interesting. He could have at least sent a photo of something or a fun-fact, but no, I didn't even get a gratuitous food pic. It was the opposite of sweeping me off my feet. He wasn't even trying. I knew enough that if the spark wasn't there from the beginning, then it isn't going to just magically show up, especially if he keeps forgetting or putting off the second date. In the end, I spent the same amount of time with him as the other dates. Goodbye Mister Egg Beard. Eck.

I had been hanging out with Mister Loner nearly every Saturday night during this time anyway. He would come over on his bike and we would cook dinner together and watch a movie. Some nights we would just drink and talk, but he never stayed over and most of the time there wasn't even a goodbye hug. I would cry every time he left. He had put me firmly in the friend zone. Mister Loner knew what he was capable of and he summed it up in a text to me once, "Sorry Babers, I am fucked."

I looked at this text a million times. During our faux-domestic bliss, I would feel maximum Zelda hearts. The six-plus hours on a Saturday night, when we were pretending to be in a relationship, were always perfect. He even had blue eyes …

Twelve

Mister Chuckles the Nurse

Carrboro, NC circa 2011

My superlative image of romance, which is something that I saw in a café in Paris while I was stuck with my family, is of a man drinking a coffee and reading a book while sitting across from a woman reading a magazine and drinking a glass of wine. They were at the same table in the same café but somehow, they had figured out how to be totally independent at the same time. I had never seen that before and I could not look away. I fell in love with that image, and that became the relationship I wanted. Mister Chuckles the Nurse thought it was romantic too, the way you can just be content with someone.

He winked first. I winked back. On Clash.com, things always started off with a wink or a dwink (a DRINK with a wink).

"It tastes different too," he said, referring to my decaf tagline. We seemed to be on the same page. No other guy had addressed these two specific things. I was beginning to feel hopeful. He could have stopped reading my profile after the tagline, since, apparently, he was busy with nursing school. But I gave him the benefit of the doubt.

After exchanging only one more email, he suggested we meet at a coffee shop that was close to me. Furthermore, it was a good one, and he noted that I lived in Carrboro and that he has been and enjoys the coffee there as well. I was encouraged. Instead of a million emails, we had arranged a date with just a few.

"I'm not looking for a pen pal, I am looking for a date," I had to tell guys before. Turns out, one dude was just looking for a pen pal or as he put it, just a friend. So, I have learned that you must be clear and direct about what you want because everyone has their own objectives, and they won't always be upfront about them. This was made clear to me after my second OkStupid date: brunch with Mister All American Preppy Teddy Bear. He had written to me— every day for a week—about mafia movies.

"You're really very lovely in person," said Mister All American Preppy Teddy Bear at the end of our first date. It felt like a dream and I wanted to believe him and that this was the beginning of something, but I knew better. I remember going to my parents' house after this date feeling depressed. I had finally, in my early 30s, experienced what I thought a date should feel like. Mister All American Preppy Teddy Bear wasn't like anyone I had ever dated before. He dressed like a frat boy but was smart, funny, and played the ukulele on a regular basis. He seemed like your typical all-American white bread dude.

In other words, I was very surprised that at our age, he was not married. Which is something I should have asked him directly and have since learned to ask on the very first date. When you're dating in your 30s, you need to look each date in the eye and ask, "Are you currently married?" Either guys laugh and say, "No, or they pause and say, welllllll, we are separated or about to get separated or things are basically over, and they have grown apart … " All just a bunch of words that mean "still married!" SDH went out on a date with a guy who did come out and tell her that he was living with his soon to be ex-wife and her girlfriend and he thought it was only fair that he had someone too (p.s. there were kids involved). Who could say no to that dream scenario?

My thought about Mister All American Preppy Teddy Bear was that he was married and just wanted to see what else was out there. After our one and only date, I never heard from him again and when I checked his profile a week and a day after our date, it had been completely erased, as if he never existed. He was careful to make sure we only communicated through OkStupid and I never got his number or email. Now, I know why. I still wonder if his wife ever found out.

The sad part is, this was not new to me. I learned this lesson in college from my friend Brett. After having spent every Thursday night together for a year, I had been shocked to learn that I should have directly asked Brett if he had a girlfriend on that very first Thursday. I knew we were just friends. We had never shared anything more than a brief hug, but it was confusing because he would send emails counting down the hours until we would meet next. To this day, I can't think of anything in my life that has made me feel more special than receiving those emails. I loved them. None of my other friends counted down the minutes until we were in each other's presence. It felt romantic. I thought we would eventually move into a romantic relationship. Brett would also say romantic things to me. "You are so great; you remind me of John Stossel" he proclaimed to me one night.

"John Stossel? The guy with the mustache from 20/20?" I had to be sure.

He said it was because I asked a lot of questions, and he liked my sarcastic streak. I never thought being interested and having a sense of humor would provoke a John Stossel comparison from male friends, at least that was never my intention.

"I love John Stossel!" I responded, thinking, "Wow, Brett really knows how to compliment me!"

While walking me home one night, he casually mentioned that his girlfriend was coming back next week. She was studying abroad for a year. I stopped walking and repeated the word "girlfriend". I asked why he had never mentioned a girlfriend before, and his response was simply that I had never asked. (I had also never asked if I reminded him of John Stossel, but anyway). Sigh. Those emails counting down the hours until our next meeting were likely misplaced and their sentiment was truly meant for his study abroad broad. So, the lesson learned from Mister All American Preppy Teddy Bear was one I had to learn twice: Look them dead in the eye and ask for the name of their wife or girlfriend. Then move on accordingly.

I've often had to learn a lesson through repetition. Even though I am a very slow learner with the paperwork to prove it (my mother had me "psychologically evaluated" in 1996 and I have hung onto the results ever since). People think that I am smarter than I actually am. It's because I had to take a placement exam before starting first grade at St. Christopher's. I cheated off of Kristen Gardner's paper. I had never taken a test before and I had no idea what to do. But Kristen seemed to know exactly what to do. I copied her answers and was put into the top track or group or whatever it was called. My entire educational life has been a lie that I have struggled to maintain. Luckily, I have always been able to surround myself with people who are smarter than me, to help maintain this facade. Whew, I have not confessed that to anyone before.

My brain is just slow, and that suits me, but it can make some social interactions a little awkward. When I am blankly staring into your eyes, hoping you don't snap at me or wave your hands in my face, what I'm actually doing is processing what you just said and formulating a response in my own time—no need to say it again.

I definitely did not want to cheat again (sorry Kristen!), let alone for my entire life. To keep up, I chose to study during almost every waking hour. By the time I was a freshman in high school, I had a bleeding ulcer. I made myself a nervous wreck. I was constantly biting my nails. Well, the nail biting started in catholic school and I still constantly bite my nails, but luckily the ulcer never came back.

So, Mister Chuckles the Nurse and I met for coffee on a Sunday night. He texted to see if I was there at the same time I texted him. We were both sitting in our cars. This makes me laugh and less nervous. However, once we sit down with our coffees, it proceeds to turn into one of the most boring conversations I have ever had in my entire life. I was thinking maybe it is a nurse thing. Was I having flashbacks to my time with the army nurse, aka Mister Vintage Horse Trough?

I was working double overtime, trying to get him to laugh, and he kept saying, "That is really funny." Then he took a sip of his coffee and looked at me, just looked, not even cracking a smile. Not once. It was so bizarre. And frustrating. He. Was. Like. A. Ro-bot.

I realize that I may not be funny to everyone, but he never even tried to be funny or clever. Perhaps he was nervous, but when I looked into his eyes, I didn't see the slightest hint of even a crow's toe, let alone a foot. It was an indicator of how this man had not laughed much in his life. I would give you an example of what I said to be funny, but you would not find it funny and side with ol' Mister Chuckles. You had to be there ... Trust me!

We need to remember that he was a nursing student, still in nursing school. On any given Sunday night he is tired and probably still has hours of studying and homework. I could feel his stress. "Should you even be here right now, on a date with me? Do we need to pull out your homework and get to work on it together? Maybe I can help? I want to help. I get it," I thought to myself as he jabbered on.

When I was in pharmacy school, it was all consuming. When I wasn't studying, I was working at Eckerd, which I loved, and when I wasn't doing either of those things, I was almost exclusively hanging out with people in my pharmacy school class, talking about pharmacy stuff. Dating Mister Ghost at the beginning of pharmacy school, I spent a lot of time telling him I was sorry. Sorry I wasn't more interesting and fun to talk to and sorry to have only pharmacy stuff to talk about over pizza as I glance at my notes next to my greasy napkin.

When Mister Ring of Fire moved back to Chapel Hill during my last year of pharmacy school, there were nights that I took my notes into a bar and I sat across from him with a coffee as he drank beer. Coincidentally, both our dads worked for IBM, and mine brought the entire family to his work building in Philadelphia one summer Sunday afternoon. He showed us that his cubicle was the only one on the whole floor. It was literally the only one and it was shocking. "This is why we have to move to North Carolina," he said. My father knew that he needed to show us for us to completely understand why we had to leave the only place any of us had ever lived, including he and my mother. I don't remember anyone saying anything as we stared at that solitary cubicle.

It was the summer before my freshman year in high school. I went from a small, private Quaker school in the suburbs of Philadelphia (think the TV sitcom *The Goldbergs*) to a humongous public high school in Chapel Hill, North Carolina. I didn't know how to laugh then either.

That all changed my senior year in high school when I met Mister Ring of Fire and his twin brother. They have the best laughs in the world and they use them constantly. They are the ones who taught me the secret to life, you create your own fun and no matter what it is, it can be fun. I say things are life-changers a lot, but this one was THE life changer. After Mister Loner met the twins for the first time, he complained to me on the way to the car that his face hurt from laughing so much. Mister Manicorn, who you will meet later on, promise, said he had never met anyone like them. They are magic to be around. They set the bar high, at magic. So, after meeting them I spent most of my life thinking it was not possible to meet anyone as funny as them or someone who made me feel the way they do. It wasn't until I was sitting a row behind them at their father's memorial service as we listened to people describe their father, as I describe them, that I realized they had learned it too. And I thought what a beautiful thing to have passed down to your children. It was the first and last time I ever saw them sad.

I learned that I needed someone who was able to make me laugh and laugh with me. It is a need. Unfortunately, it did not appear as if Mister Chuckles the Nurse was capable of even a smile. I thought he could have learned to laugh by being around me, but we were both knocking on the door of our mid-thirties, so could he change? Did he want to change? Could he change my mind? I was ready to go (not interested in another bleeding ulcer). This was such a deal breaker for me that I never even considered bringing out the conversation cards.

As we were walking towards the door, I saw my friend Lilli was sitting nearby with her roommate. I didn't even pause for an introduction. I quickly said hello with my eyes wide, giving them everything they needed to know in one look. After we unceremoniously ended the date and separated, I drove around the building and came back in to sit with Lilli and her roommate, sighing heavily as I sat down.

"Med student or nursing student?" they asked. I was shocked at their accuracy. Turns out they had seen him in the Health Sciences Library and were watching us the entire time. They knew it didn't go well.

Not too long before this, I was at Lilli's house with SDH for an apron party. One of her good friends had made a bunch of aprons with her Mom and she and her roommate were hosting a party to help sell them. SDH and I arrived an hour late. They were dancing around—music blaring—in nothing but aprons and underwear. Maybe they thought no one would show up for their apron party. I wouldn't have missed it. It was an awesome scene to walk into, but now SDH and I felt like we were intruding. They turned down the music and changed and sat down with us as we looked at the aprons. I bought a pile of aprons for me and for gifts and there were a couple handmade purses that I grabbed because I felt bad for being late and intruding. Soon other friends arrived and we ate and drank and talked online-dating. While SDH and I were relaying our escapades, one apron party attendee admitted to making a spreadsheet to track the online dating exploits of her and her friends. SDH and I looked at each other, "Why didn't we think of that?"

A spreadsheet might sound like overkill, but dating in a small town while your friends are also actively dating can lead to some overlap. A spreadsheet could be a helpful resource. Lilli and her roommate were also single and dating, but, for Lilli at least, online dating had yet to enter the picture. I'm sure the conversation was not encouraging, and seeing me bomb at Open Eye Cafe with Mister Chuckles the Nurse probably didn't help either.

One time, after Lilli had broken up with this potter, SDH and I were shopping for local treasures post-brunch when SDH noticed a mug made by Lilli's potter ex-boyfriend. She got my attention and showed me his name and then raised the mug above her head and pretended like she was about to smash it on the ground. We were both laughing hysterically as she proposed that we smash all of the pottery he had for sale in the tiny shop. The woman behind the counter was nervously looking over at us, the only two customers in the store.

We were in her store almost every week, buying this or that. We were regulars. She probably felt she knew us, but you think you know someone and then suddenly they come into your store threatening to smash hundreds of dollars' worth of pottery, so you get worried. She looked worried. She must have thought we had too many brunch cocktails. The truth is, we mostly just had coffee—there's a North Carolina law barring the sale of alcohol before noon on Sundays. It was for the best. We all had shit to do anyway.

After a different sober Sunday brunch that had ended before noon, we were on the sidewalk noting the time, saying goodbye, and realizing we had the entire day ahead of us when Crafty yelled, "The oyster is my world!" inverting the expression as she is known to do.

"You lucky son of a bitch!" SDH responded, and then we parted ways. This is how we brunched.

Crafty's first language is English, but you would never know that. She is constantly searching for English words or confusing common idioms. She is fluent in Spanish, having lived and played rugby in Salamanca, Spain, for a year during college. Also, when we were in high school and not close friends yet, she had a surgery done that was supposed to correct a slight speech impediment. Sometimes Crafty sounded British. She had lived all over the country as a child and maybe no regional accent was given enough time to stick, but she definitely never lived in the United Kingdom. After the oral surgeon snipped her frenum (that thin piece of skin perpendicular to the underside of your tongue that keeps it attached to the bottom of your mouth; hers was overdeveloped to the point where she could barely stick her tongue out past her teeth), she basically spoke normally. The oyster being our world became our mantra. I even have it tattooed on my back, in cursive, over a giant black and white open oyster.

Meanwhile, back at the shop, after a few more minutes of bad mouthing the mug, it was placed safely back on the shelf with its friends. We bought some greeting cards and left. We visited his pottery every week after that, smiling and commenting that it looked like it was all still there. That was almost better than smashing it.

I waited a few days after the humorless Mister Chuckles the Nurse date before texting him my usual line that I am not the girl for him.

"Well, I am sad to hear that. I saw this glimmer of something really special in you. Any man would be very fortunate to have you come into his life. I wish you the best of luck in your search," he said. Ugh, he was such a nice guy, if only he had learned how to laugh.

Thirteen

Mister Constantly Smoking Pastry Chef

Carrboro, NC circa 2011

I was still hanging out with Mister Loner, on and off, and listening to a song by Wavves featuring Best Coast: "Nodding Off." It's from their Life Sux EP. At that time, I didn't know what to call Mister Loner or what role he was playing in my life. I just knew he STILL wasn't … ready. I needed to move on but that day I fled the beach, was just a glint in my eye.

I heard that Nathan, the lead singer of Wavves, was dating Bethany from Best Coast—apparently, they wrote "Nodding Off" together. If this song was about them, it sounded to me like they were struggling in their relationship. At least they could write a song about it together. I was stuck birdwatching, in silence of course, with Mister Loner once a week. Silently birding (and brooding) wasn't helping me to work out any of my frustrations. If anything, it was causing more.

I had been looking at birds for months and I could not identify a single Tufted Titmouse! Not one! To this day, Mister Manicorn will ask me to identify birds and I always have to remind him, as he laughs, that I am retired. Thank goodness! But, I'm getting ahead of myself. So, I would listen to "Nodding Off" at volume 50, screaming all the words and feeling better. However, being the slow learner I am, I continued waiting patiently for Mister Loner to come around. While I foolishly waited for Mister Loner to realize that we should get back together, I kept myself entertained by dating.

Enter Mister Constantly Smoking Pastry Chef. He is OKStupid date number one and lives down the street from Mister Loner and Crafty, and across the street from SDH. He does not drive nor own a car. This was revealed to me as I was giving him a ride home after our first date. He was supposed to be my escape from Mister Loner, but already he was worse. I was immediately forced to take care of him. He suggested that we meet at The Crunkleton, a cocktail bar named after the bowtie-wearing owner Mr. Crunkleton.

The Crunkleton greets you with dark wood, leather, and hundreds and hundreds of back lit liquor bottles on glass shelves, like an altar for alcoholics. The first time SDH and I sat at the bar, she looked at all the bottles and had flashbacks to when she bartended and had to wipe down all the bottles and glass shelves every night. Suddenly, they didn't look so pretty or spiritual. Every night? Yikes! Anyway, I was happy that Mister Constantly Smoking Pastry Chef picked this particular bar because I knew from previous experience that I will have a pretty good chance of getting a decent dirty martini. Obtaining the perfect dirty martini is never a guarantee, no matter where you are. I have even let myself down numerous times. There are just way too many variables. So, when it does happen, it feels like magic.

"Oh, by the way, I hope it's ok that I smoke," the Chef said, after having already lit a cigarette as we stood outside the entrance to The Crunkleton.

In my OkStupid preferences, I made the mistake of saying that it didn't matter to me if someone smoked. I didn't want to exclude anyone for something that seemed, at the time, like a relatively small life choice (especially in North Carolina), like preferring red or white wine. Having never dated someone that smoked cigarettes, I was naive. I didn't respond to the Chef right away, so he pointed out that he knew he didn't include "smoker" in his profile but saw that I had expressed no preference in mine. So, there we were on what would be the first of countless smoke breaks.

I guess I could have ended the date there and gone home. That is certainly what my hairdresser would have done. But I had already secured all the bobby pins to my hair, applied nail stickers, and glossed up my lips. I was so close to a martini I could smell the olive brine. I don't like wasting food, alcohol, or expensive lip gloss, so it was time to accept his smoking and move on.

Inside, he revealed, to my absolute delight, that he also drinks martinis, and so martinis in-hand we settle down to get to know each other. Out of nowhere, a guy I was barely friends with in high school comes in and, just when I think he will never notice or remember me, yells my entire name across the bar. He is already drunk and wants to take this time to catch up. I am trying hard to throw in the fact that I am on a first date and this is not really a good time, but this takes a while. By the time I manage to get away and rejoin Mister Constantly Smoking Pastry Chef, he suggests that we head to Lantern—where the bar in the back is my favorite spot-on earth. I enthusiastically agree, but he is already almost out the door, cigarette between his fingers. I think he would have gone there with or without me.

Almost as soon as we sat down, several of Mister Constantly Smoking Pastry Chef's "good friends" showed up. It was unclear if this was a coincidence or if he sent an SOS text. His crew consisted of males and females of the generic hipster variety. I felt like I had seen them all around Carrboro before. They were so excited to see each other and he kept telling me, as they ordered food and drinks, that they were his "really good friends". If you have to tell me several times that you are all really good friends, then perhaps you are not *really good friends*? It was so strange. There were three or four of them, I am not sure, it all happened so fast. They swarmed and started to ask questions. I felt like I was getting to know them more than I was Mister Constantly Smoking Pastry Chef. He didn't even try to talk to me. I ordered another martini and sipped it slowly as one of his male friends, who was sitting next to me (with these huge, thick-rimmed, black, hipster glasses), started asking me questions. His hipster face was way too close to mine. It was hard for my eyes to focus on him and not have double vision. He wanted to know where I worked and what I did and where I hung out. He didn't seem to realize or know that Mister Constantly Smoking Pastry Chef and I were on a first date. When I shared this with him, he switched gears and started telling me how great Mister Constantly Smoking Pastry Chef was. As he was praising him, I looked over to see to whom my date was talking. He wasn't even at the table anymore; out for another smoke break. Mister Generic Hipster Glasses and I got to know each other pretty well that night. He was the one who introduced me to the other ladies at the table. I didn't talk to Mister Constantly Smoking Pastry Chef at all, except when he asked me for a ride home.

As I drove him home, he said he hoped it was ok that his friends had joined us and kept explaining that he was really very close with his friends. There he goes again asking me if something is ok after it is already happening. He made it sound like they couldn't possibly have a night away from one other. I have close friends too, who would have known that I was on a first date with someone and acted accordingly. I left that last part unsaid.

The Chef told me that he would think of a place for our next date and be in touch. He texted me later in the week saying he knew of an exclusive place where we could have dinner. "Watch it be his house," I muttered to myself.

It was! He invited me over to his house to cook a steak dinner, having remembered that during one of the few times we had spoken, I'd told him my favorite meal was a dirty martini and a rare steak. At least he was thoughtful. I debated going. It didn't seem like a safe choice. I consulted with Crafty and SDH and they said they would both be home and would check on me. So, I agreed to a second date.

I arrived at his house in my black cowboy boots, the same dress I wore on my date with Mister Wizard (the loudly-patterned, blue and black, short-sleeved dress that the secretary at work thought was too short), my hair in an updo with a million colorful bobby pins, the AstroTurf purse, and an additional bag slung over my shoulder containing my electronic martini shaking machine and accoutrement.

I rang the doorbell and when it opened, I was greeted by a total of five women (count 'em, FIVE), clad in their finest lounge wear, watching *True Blood* and, now, looking at me. No one said hello, or anything. I started to panic. Was I in the wrong house? I was trying to remember Mister Constantly Smoking Pastry Chef's real name when he walked in and broke the silence. He made introductions with a big smile.

Surprise! Old-what's-his-name lives with five women who all appear to be younger than him, much younger than him. He tells me later that it works out because he cooks for them. They seem suspicious of me, especially of the fact that I arrived with a machine and supplies to make martinis. To be clear, I didn't buy this machine. It was a wedding gift given to my sister Katie from our 90-something-year-old relative who loves an appletini but no longer has the wrist or arm strength to make them herself. She can't live without her electronic martini making machine and so she doesn't know how others are living without it either. Alas, my sister and her husband drink beer, so they gave it to me.

Some of the roommates left or went to other rooms as he gave me a quick tour, ending in the kitchen. The strangest part of the tour is that he takes me upstairs to see his bedroom, like a little kid. This was the first thing he showed me. He didn't take me there to steal a kiss or have some alone time with me, but to stand there proudly and show me his very basic bedroom. It was like a bed and a closet. I took note that his bed was made. But what did he want me to say? Good job, your room is clean? I briefly thought about using the cheesy line from MTV Cribs that almost everyone uses as they bring you to their bedroom, "Is this where the magic happens?" but decided against it, in case he hadn't watched every episode of MTV Cribs as I had. I gave him a generic and somewhat enthusiastic "Nice!" That was the one and only time I was ever in his bedroom.

As I made our first martini, one roommate joined us while she was waiting for her boyfriend to pick her up. She looked like your typical bowhead (grown women/students who walk around with giant bows in their hair like they are five years old), which is a term I lovingly use to describe these women who most often also choose to pay for their friends by joining a UNC sorority. Chef asked the roommate where they were going. She answered him while keeping her eyes on me the whole time, as I unpacked the jalapeño-stuffed olives, Pinnacle vodka, dry vermouth in an olive oil sprayer, and plastic cocktail toothpicks the shape of nails.

"What are you making?" she asks, starting to laugh. As I start to explain, thankfully her boyfriend shows up in loafers with no socks and I knew she had met her perfect Chad or Brad, who whisked her away before I could answer. When our martinis are ready, it is time to go outside to a picnic bench in the yard for a cigarette. I joined him on all these smoke breaks, and he took me to a different location each time, so that I could experience different parts of the rental property. As we were moving around, playing a sort of musical smoking chairs, his roommates came out to say hi or ask a question about what he was making for dinner. They let us know what they would be studying or going out to do for the rest of the night—like I asked. I was trying to have a moment alone with him. I was also getting constant texts from SDH and Crafty. They could see me outside on the front porch, so they knew I was alive. But was I having a good time? Then I started to worry that since Crafty and SDH could see me, then maybe Mister Loner could too. Or maybe he'd roll by on his bike?

We were never alone for long. Dinner took forever. Every time I turned around, we were on another smoke break. When the food was finally ready, he invited one of his sporty, young roommates to eat with us. She was dressed in athletic shorts and a t-shirt. She sat next to him. I may as well have been a ghost. Was he trying to make me jealous? Does he like her? Is he trying to make her jealous by having me there? Why would he not be alone with me?

My "rare steak" was almost well done. Maybe that's why he'd hardly spoken to me. He knew he had failed me. I did not point out the status of the steak because he must have already known, having both paid for and cooked it—about as well as he had cooked the sad, bland, mushy broccolini. It was a free meal, after all, so I praised him and his cooking abilities and reminded myself that, to be fair, he had made it clear he was a pastry chef.

After dinner we sat on the back porch, a place I had not yet been for a smoke break, and I found myself grateful that all the roommates were either out or had checked in and told us what they were doing in other parts of the house, so we were finally alone and I could relax. Plus, we were not on the front porch where Mister Loner could potentially see us. I had previously told him about my conversation cards, so he told me to bring them outside, but first he started with the dreaded wife interview, about our potential future together, and then mocking my answer.

He asked where I saw myself living, and I answered, Carrboro. I started to explain that it is close to my parents, that I have a job and friends that I love here, a townhome that I own ... But I never get to say all that because he interrupts, "You just see yourself living in Carrboro? Forever?" and then laughs. I start looking around and praying for a roommate to show up.

He had had a lucrative job out in California, complete with an art collection and car that he'd lost during the financial crisis. He was in North Carolina starting over. I tell him to pick a conversation card and, of course, it is a non-PG one. "Where is the craziest place you ever had sex?" To that point, my experiences with sex had been extremely limited.

"Nowhere crazy, huh? You've just had sex in a bed, with the lights off?" He has a grin on his face the entire time. He tells me about a time he had sex outside on top of a building. I think I cringed the whole time he was telling the story. I don't care how many martinis I had, sex in public with a chance of falling off a building sounds terrifying. I know he was just trying to make himself feel better with his answers and by putting me down, but that showed me what type of person he was. Maybe this is why he didn't want to be alone with me, he didn't even want to be alone with himself. It was time to leave. He didn't try for a sneak-attack-kiss or even a hug. I never got to smell what it would be like to be with a smoker. I thank him for cooking again, because I don't know what else to say, and add that I will be in touch.

Yeah, right.

I text SDH and Crafty that I am alive but full of negative hearts. He reminded me so much of Mister Loner but without the charm. Instead of waving all the red flags away, this time I heeded them. Progress?! I never even used my line about not being the right girl for him because he was never in touch again. I continued to remain in violation of our three-date rule while changing my preference on OkStupid to nonsmokers. Much like white wine, smokers and insecure assholes are not for me.

Fourteen

Mister Father of Five

Chapel Hill, NC circa 2012

Valentine's Day was just *behind the door,* as my friend Irina says, and NPR was airing love stories as I was getting ready for my date. I foolishly took that as a sign that the universe was preparing me for what was immediately to come: *my* love story!

The man on the radio said the key to finding love was to never give up hope. Radio man was talking directly to me, no doubt, especially when he said, "Hold out for the real deal, it is worth it!" With those words echoing in my ear, I headed out for my third OkStupid date, practically bursting with hope.

"Set low expectations," Mike from work always advised. But, did this go against my current gratuitous hope strategy? Was hope … bad? Mike has been married for 40-plus years, to the same woman. They are still in love and miraculously seemed to really like each other too. They gave me hope. Expectations be damned! A man like Mike was out there for me.

My expectations were, in reality, dropping with each date, but I couldn't help but get excited before each one. I blame it on my Hope Dies Last tattoo.

Rubywooilicious. That was my OKStupid screen name. Not surprisingly, it resulted in many men calling me Ruby. I didn't correct them. The name comes from a classic red MAC lipstick: Ruby Woo. In my search for the perfect red, I came across it but fell more in love with the name than the shade. The last part was added because I thought it would help me seem delightful, plus there were already several Ruby Woos out there on OKStupid and I didn't want to take a number.

"It's important to have a fake name," said my friend Katie Wilson. "It should spring from your mouth as easily as your real name." I learned this when I was 12 while on a beach trip with Katie, her family, and one of her new friends. I was the old friend. Since I had just moved from Philly where she still lived, I didn't know this new friend. This new friend was exciting and beautiful and brought a lot of male-attention to us as we strolled down the boardwalk one night. That's when my fake name was born.

We didn't want to be rude and not give our names, but we also didn't want to give our real names to potential woo-ers. It felt safer to go with aliases and way more fun. I tried out Anne and Sara but they didn't feel right, so my standard fake name is Claire, for my best friend at St. Christopher Catholic School. I liked it so much, I picked Claire as my confirmation name too, so now my standard fake is officially part of my name, at least in the eyes of the Catholic Church.

I met Mister Father of Five at Fosters in Chapel Hill where we both drank large coffees and talked for exactly two hours over no food. He had a faux hawk, small holes in his ears where earrings used to be, and a tattoo on his arm that he had designed. The fact that he didn't have earrings in was depressing. I don't think men with pierced ears can win. If they don't have earrings in, then it's a sign their youth is behind them, and, if they have earrings in as an older man, it's like, "Who do you think you are, Harrison Ford?" An earring looks depressing even on Harrison Ford. If Indiana Jones can't pull it off, why are you even trying?

His tattoo: a broken heart made of two red lightning bolts. "I wear my heart on my sleeve," he said proudly. I knew better.

Mister Loner had wanted black hearts tattooed on his arm and never got them. He drew them on each day. The more this guy talked, the more he felt like Mister Loner II, and the more I felt like we were in a serious broken-heart situation. My feelings were confirmed as he summarized:

"I have five kids. I had two kids with my first wife before she died. My first two kids had to endure the loss of our family dog along with their mother. My second wife cheated on me. I have not had much luck on OkStupid."

This was a lot to take in.

With every new detail, my hopefulness was depleted. "Did his profile mention five kids?!" I thought with desperation. He also lets me know that he skateboards and plays the guitar. Essentially, he's Mister Loner the sequel, plus five kids.

Hello God, it's me, Mary. Why hath you forsaken meeee?

His profile did state that he is an artist and that he wishes he could earn a living by just being an artist. I asked him about this and exactly what type of artist he was. He responded: "Painting, I think, or drawing, or both."

Huh? I thought.

"Have you seen *Exit Through the Gift Shop*?" he said, as I was becoming disoriented. "Yes, yes I have."

"That's more like what I do."

"How do you mean?"

"I make a bunch of stencils with famous people wearing the hats worn by the rock band DEVO. You may have seen them spray painted around town. I have a friend of a friend who does PR for DEVO, and he says they might be interested in them."

OK.

As he spoke more about ... his art, it sounded like he wouldn't pursue it even though it seemed like the only way he could imagine making money—off his illegal street art. Did I need to remind this man he was in his thirties and has five kids?

Inevitably, he brought up *The Big Lebowski.*

"I don't drink much, but I used to always drink White Russians, so I could be like The Dude," he shared.

Drinking the same beverage as a fictional character is how he was trying to be interesting? Plus, all that heavy cream mixed with alcohol? Yuck.

Then, "I thought you wouldn't go out with me because you're tall." I probably rolled my eyes. How many insecurities are we going to have to run through on the first date? Maybe he was trying to get them all out of the way? I reassured him: "Oh, height doesn't matter to me. My friend Julie is significantly taller than her husband and they are perfectly happy despite everyone feeling the need to point out their height difference."

Did he have a faux hawk to give himself added height? Maybe he thought it made him more interesting? And then: "I don't know who I am. Do you know who you are?"

"No," I said quickly, not wanting to make him feel bad. I had had enough conversations like this with Mister Loner that included him crying. I did not want to make this man, this father of five, cry. Sigh.

But, yes I know exactly who I am. I'm Mary. I come from a long line of them and I survived Hebrew, Catholic, Quaker, and pharmacy schools.

A two-arm, full-body hug. That's how Mister Father of Five left me. It didn't feel creepy. It was actually rather cathartic. I felt like we just had a therapy session of sorts, and no conversation cards were needed! The date might have been rated a relative success (meaning not in the negative Zelda heart range) until I decided to post to Facebook. Chalk it up to my incessant hopefulness.

"Third OKStupid date went really well, but he has five kids and two previous wives. Too much baggage??" The responses I got from my friends and family were an assortment of:

"Def too much baggage."

"Is he rich?"

"That means he's both lovable and fertile, what more can you ask for???"

"Um ... Honey, no."

"Means he knows how to charm a woman into commitment and then leave them with the ball and chains. I vote no"

"A lot of baggage, but as long as there is no baby mama drama, you might be ok!"

"Are these divorces and kids real or in his head?"

Five kids was not a deal breaker for me. Should it have been? We will never know. But, in the end, it wasn't the five kids and two previous wives that made me not go out with him again. It was the baggage of his broken heart. I had learned from Mister Loner that someone else's broken heart was way too much for me to carry.

After the date, I headed to the PTA thrift store for some retail therapy. They had one wall dedicated to Valentine's Day with random red items, heart-shaped whatevers, and a red scarf tacked to the wall. I spotted the second edition of my Heart-to-Heart conversation cards. I didn't even know there was a second edition. What luck! "Yes!" I said, under my breath as much as possible. I really needed these cards. There would be many more dates to come.

Fifteen

Mister B

Chapel Hill, NC circa 2012

I'm not sure how it happens or what it means, but a disproportionate number of men I have dated, including the Manicorn, have a name that starts with the letter B. I didn't pay attention to all the Bs until my sister Katie's friend, Vanessa, was excitedly describing a guy she was going to date and when she finally said his full name out loud, we realized that his name contained exactly six B's, so he became known as B6. He ended up being such a whirlwind that when it ended, she told me to beware of men with so many Bs in their name. They will only break your heart.

Mister Loner, my first Clash date, had a screen name of B1000 and a first name that started with a B. When I texted Vanessa with this information, she told me to brace myself. I put him in my phone as B1000 to remind myself of all the Bs he came with and that is how he remained in my phone.

I blame this particular Mister B on the *dwinking*. Crafty coined the term and taught me the technique. She would get drunk and then just wink at everyone she could on Clash and see who would wink back. She did not have much luck with her dwinking on Clash, so she tried OkStupid. Turns out, that's where her future husband/baby daddy was hiding—with another name riddled with B's.

Crafty had been out with Bobby all night long when she showed up at my house for our early morning flight to New York City for my birthday. She was all smiles and full of words about this man—she had met her Manicorn. He was a PhD student studying East German Literature, specifically suicides. Who knew? I had hooked Mister B after applying Crafty's dwinking strategy to my own love life. Since Mister B's screen name only contained one B, I thought he would be safe. In actuality, he would be the person who made me deactivate my Clash.com profile.

While trying to get to the open seat next to me at a large, oppressively decorated brunch spot, Mister B, after having assessed the situation, shouted across the restaurant to me, "I feel as if there is already something between us!" I laughed, shrugged, and just enjoyed the fact that he was witty and talkative—no conversation cards needed.

On a first date, conversations develop that I don't normally have, or I talk about things I don't usually do, like on my first date with Mister Loner. I talked about my friend being murdered, which is not something I ever talk about. Nathalee was one of my pharmacy interns and we spent a lot of time together in and outside the pharmacy. She ate chips like no one I ever met. She ate them one by one and would describe each one after she ate it. "That one was so fresh!" I can still hear her exclaiming.

I was away on vacation one summer when I missed a call from her and didn't immediately call her back. During the next few days, I received several voicemails from her reminding me I had not called her back yet. They all ended with her asking if I was raised by wolves—click. When I called her back, she just wanted to know how my vacation was going.

I knew that she wanted to get a huge red dragon tattoo that stretched across the back of her petite frame. Roaming around Target, she would see someone with a tattoo on their back and go up to them and start asking a million questions. Did it hurt? When did you get it? Has it faded? Are you happy with it there? She did this a lot. I thought the red dragon suited her personality perfectly, but she died before she could get her tattoo. I got a small dragon with one red eye tattooed on my hip after that, so she is always with me. I am not sure why or how she came up, but it led to a very awkward pause and me trying not to cry. He whispered "rainbows and puppy dogs" under his breath. It made me smile and we were able to move on.

With Mister B, I talked about God. In fact, I could not shut up about Her. I had recently started going to church again and signed up for this women's book club through the church. We met once a week. Trying to process all this new religious stuff was overwhelming. Mister B was a philosophy major, which served to fuel our religion talk. I had never met one of those before, let alone been on a date with one. I was enjoying flying free without my conversation cards.

I agreed to a second date with Mister B because of an Ally McBeal type-hallucination I had during a Toubab Krewe show at the Cat's Cradle. As I was enjoying a sugar-free Red Bull and my first exposure to Toubab Krewe's incredible instrumental music, I started to have a trippy vision. I was watching myself dance with some man I didn't recognize, and we appeared to be in wedding gear. I felt this enormous sense of peace and happiness that I had never felt before. It was like I was dreaming while awake. I didn't want it to end!

Could Mister B be my hallucinated groom? He did have dark hair and eyes with glasses ... I needed more time to figure it out.

We ended up at a small Italian restaurant for our second date, only because the Indian place he suggested was closed. I suggested the Italian place since Mister B had no plan B. Why would I expect plan B when plan A wasn't even properly thought out or researched?

We were walking down Franklin Street together when he admitted that he probably should have checked their website. Sigh. I am someone who plans. I can't help it. I need the illusion I am in control. I'd been to this restaurant several times and I loved how they made you feel like you were in someone's home, so I felt like it would be the perfect quiet place to sit and have a nice leisurely meal. We settled in at a table for two and suddenly he was not talkative. He dropped his napkin so many times that he spent more time under the table than talking to me. It was so bizarre and incredibly annoying. We needed God on this date, but I had promised not to bring Her up. It was like Mister B was more nervous on this date than the first one. He did not drink, but told me that I could (Oh, thanks for the permission!). I had never been around someone who didn't drink on a date. I didn't know how to react. Do I drink or not drink? I started off not drinking because he wasn't (the sacrifices we make for men!).

As we were sitting in silence not drinking alcohol, we watched the chef come out of the kitchen with a ladder and tool box, still dressed in his chef whites, in an effort to make a repair to the front door. Our waitress came over to confirm what I already knew: our dinner was going to be super delayed because of the door situation. Cue Mister B dropping his napkin, again, and me ordering a glass of wine.

After dinner we made our way to the Franklin Hotel lounge. There was no one there besides us, the bartender, and a one-man band. When I say a one-man band, it was literally just a man with a keyboard who sang sometimes. I needed a martini.

Mister B said I should sit in one of the comfy leather chairs and he would order my drink. I tell him my order, "an extra-dirty vodka martini with Kettle One, Absolut if they don't have Kettle One, and extra olives, if possible, please". He panicked.

"I don't drink so I don't know what that means when you say extra dirty and it feels weird to say that and I don't want to screw that up so you better get it yourself," he spewed back at me.

There used to be this incredibly cute bartender at The Station in Carrboro who would cover his face and turn red every time I asked for a dirty martini. He could never look me in the eye when asking, "How dirty do you want it?" I have learned to spare the bartender and just go ahead and say extra dirty up front instead of following up with the response, "I want it filthy!"

I asked Mister B what he wanted to drink and he just wanted a Coke. Maybe I sounded mean, but I laughed. When I dated Mister Ghost, I was not yet 21 but he was of age. So, if we were out at a bar, I would ask for a Coke. He mocked me for it. "You could have anything to drink and you just want a Coke?" He told me that he felt stupid giving his drink order and then asking for a Coke. I found his struggle mortifying. I really just wanted several regular fountain Cokes. What a dream come true! My mother was very restrictive with soda and sweets growing up, so to me a Coke was pretty damn special. And as soon as we could drive, my sister Katie and I would spend all of our baby-sitting money on candy. I started working at Eckerd the summer before pharmacy school and I would buy all the discounted candy I could afford and keep it hidden in a bowling bag in my closet. It wasn't until I found my dad's mini-Hershey bar stash in his car that I decided to let him in on my bowling bag secret. It would become a common occurrence for me to walk into my room and find either my dad or my sisters quietly rooting through the bag and helping themselves. So, Mister B's request for a Coke brought me back to a simpler time, when I didn't have a traumatizing drink order.

I wasn't the girl for this B either. I didn't think I could handle feeling guilty for every drink I had in his presence. I am sure that in time I would have not felt the same way or perhaps stopped drinking all together (or not) and we would have enjoyed endless Cokes together. We will never know!

Mister B found me a year later on OkStupid and sent me a message that said he wanted to check-in to see if I had any dating success. He asked me what other sites I had tried and what I had thought of them. He never asked me out again and I was happy to share what I had done and learned in the year of online dating since we'd met. He did the same for me. Finally, we wished each other good luck because we both knew how much we each needed it.

Sixteen

Mister Superficial

Circa 2012

Mister Superficial entered my life for free, courtesy of OkStupid. We never met, but he hooked me with his first message: "How do you think they will deal with the ending of *Dexter's* last season?" This was a great opening question. I was interested in him immediately. I, of course, didn't know how they would end it, but I had some thoughts. He was the only person—in or outside my dating life—that had asked me this question. All my friends were a season behind, so I was eager to commiserate on this topic.

If there is one thing I love, it's *Dexter*. And if there are two things I love, the other would be talking about *Dexter*. At one point, I had hosted a viewing party at my house every Sunday night, complete with a different blood splatter cake and blood orange cocktails. Of all the beautiful things Martha Stewart creates, I treasure her blood splatter cake stencil most.

For those who have never had the pleasure of watching *Dexter*, the title character is a blood splatter expert by day and a murderer by night that kills by a code. Dexter only kills people who he feels deserve it because he has proof, so you end up rooting for him and his bloody brand of justice. The beginning sequence of every episode is a long, detailed breakfast scene where he makes hand-squeezed blood orange juice. Ironically, *Dexter* is what brought me back to church.

My cubicle mate at work, Allyson, didn't watch *Dexter,* but that didn't stop me from telling her all about it. One day, she could not wait to tell me that the new pastor at her church loved and PREACHED *Dexter.* This I had to hear. Dexter, in season six, meets The Doomsday Killer who is a serial killer who also kills with a purpose: to enact the Doomsday Tableaus to bring about the end of days according to the Book of Revelation. In essence, it was The Doomsday Killer thinking he was executing "God's plan" versus Dexter, an atheist, working by his own code. I was interested in hearing more, so after years away from any house of worship, I headed back to church, thanks to *Dexter.*

After Mister Superficial and I got through all the *Dexter* chitchat, he asked to see more pictures of me, which, at the time, seemed like a reasonable request since I only had one picture up on my profile and I had been meaning to add more. When he asked me to go to the beach (giving me one day's notice) because a friend of his had backed out, I started to see something waving at me from a distance. It looked like it could be a red flag.

I declined the invitation and we started texting back and forth about our weekend plans. I told him that I had gotten a haircut and he asked me for a pic. Maybe he was interested, but it seemed like another photo-on-demand. I told him to enjoy the beach and proposed that we meet for brunch the following Sunday since he told me he wasn't available to meet up at all during the week.

At first, he agreed to the brunch but then suggested that we go swimming after. I would never think about even looking at water for at least an hour after eating because of my mother. Growing up, she would repeatedly tell my sisters and I the story of her grandfather, who jumped in the water for a swim directly after eating lunch on a boat with his family. He got a cramp and drowned. Astonishingly, no one on the boat was able to swim. My great-grandmother lost everything because, at that time, women couldn't own property. This is how my mother ruled, by scare tactics. Her stories were very effective, on me at least. The moral of this one is to never ever go swimming after eating because you could lose EVERYTHING.

"I don't have access to a pool," I texted, apprehensively.

"There's a pool I know of by NC State that we can use," he replied immediately and vaguely, making me wonder if he was lying and was still a student, or worse, he wasn't a student but still hung out at the pool hitting on students. I was seeing nothing but red flags.

In less than a week of texting, he had tried for more pictures and to get me to the beach and to the pool. To make matters more confusing, he asked me to find a place in Cary to have brunch. I don't live in Cary and if the pool is by NC State, then that is Raleigh, so why the hell are we having brunch in Cary? I realized that I wasn't going on this date, but I wasn't sure of my next move. I couldn't say my normal line because we hadn't even met, so that wouldn't make sense. What I should have texted him was, "If you want a girl who likes wearing a bikini, then I am definitely not the girl for you!" But I was too much of a coward to be this direct. He continued to text me, asking me about my day.

I am not the type of person who requires a check-in. I find the practice totally tedious, annoying, and a waste of time. Text me something interesting, random, or funny any time, but getting a text that reads, "I am good, and Saturday was alright," makes me want to delete your number. When he was not demanding pictures, he would send a series of these snooze fest texts that never went anywhere. Turns out, the only thing interesting about him was our shared interest in *Dexter*. This is not something that Crafty would authorize as our mutual penetration.

In pharmacy school, I had a classmate who was tall, wore red pants on occasion, and smelled amazing. He was president of his fraternity and my hypothesis was that he had so many women in his life that he couldn't remember everyone's name, so he called every female "Babe". I knew it was wrong on many levels, but I loved it when he called *me* Babe. Call me Miss Superficial! I called him "The Dish" but only behind his back. He was fascinating to me. The Dish seemed like the king of this other world I was not a part of. I had never even been inside a frat house or a frat party and there he would be, sitting on a giant bench in front of his Greek-lettered castle holding court.

I would pass him on my way to my favorite coffee shop to study. He would always wave but it was because he had manners. The Dish would always say, "Bless you," after anyone sneezed. He was not interested in getting to know me. Hell, half the time I wasn't sure he could place me. One day after an exam, we were photographed walking together. We happened to finish the test at the same time. The photo was printed in *The Daily Tarheel*, UNC's highly-circulated student newspaper. From then on, I felt like I was living my own version of the movie *She's All That* and he was going to realize one day, that despite appearances, this nameless, nearby babe was the girl for him. I had been right under his nose the entire time!

In our *Daily Tar Heel* pic, which was captioned, "Rainy Day People," he is frat-tastically dressed, even in his rain gear, and is looking down, both literally and sentimentally, complete with hands in his pockets. It's a sharp contrast to me in my "lucky pants" and rain gear, complete with umbrella and huge grin. I wore these "lucky" track pants every time I took a test. You can't tell from the picture, but they have rainbow stripes going down the sides. They became "lucky" the morning I wore them to my organic chemistry final after a night at the Cat's Cradle. G-Love and Special Sauce were playing and, in the past, despite my best efforts, I was never able to catch them live, so I had to go. I would leave early and heavily prepare for the exam in advance. This plan may seem overly cautious, but I had failed organic chemistry the first time around and my pharmacy school advisor told me that all I needed to do was get an A the second time and I would get into the pharmacy school. She made it sound so easy as she smiled, "but if you don't get an A, then you will not get into pharmacy school." It was just that simple. My entire future as a pharmacist was on the line. That's all.

I studied and then went to the concert, but could not bring myself to leave early. The exam was at 8 AM the next morning, so in order to maximize my sleep time, I wore the same clothes I wore to the concert, smelling like you do when you don't shower and are in a place where smoking is allowed indoors. I ended up getting the highest grade in the class. I had attended every single supplementary instruction section this time around. The TAs were all very familiar with me; I was often the only one there. They knew what was at stake for me too, so one of the TAs e-mailed me as soon as she graded my exam. From that day forward, I wore those track pants on exam days.

I had been trying to spend more time with Mister Dish, to get to know him outside of our pharmacy school bubble. But, every time we had these one-on-one moments, I realized he never had anything interesting or funny to say. I would try and ask him to do non-pharmacy school related outings, but he was always too busy and it became painfully clear that I was not the girl for him.

Some of my pharmacy school friends would join me for a Thursday night dinner at my parent's house and we had talked about Mister Dish so much that my dad became all too familiar with the situation. When Dad saw him for the first time at graduation, he could not wait to inform me that Mister Dish was not handsome, he was, "just tall". He wasn't sure why I had made such a big deal about this man. It made me laugh because my Dad said it, as he does with everything, directly and with such certainty.

After pharmacy school, as I sat in my dad's green Pontiac Bonneville on my first Nokia cell phone, Mister Dish and I had one last conversation. I told him where I got my first job as a pharmacist and he told me where he was working. We wished each other good luck starting our lives as pharmacists. I thought that was going to be all she wrote, but, because of the magic of Facebook, we are now virtual friends who never comment or message each other, and I can see his major life milestones. I saw when he finally found a Babe whose name I am assuming he was able to remember and married her. Of course, I looked at the wedding pictures and when I saw the same Nicole Miller bridesmaid dress in the thrift store months later, in my size, I could not help myself and tried it on. It didn't fit and I laughed at myself in the dressing room. That was not my life! However, he is now living in the same town I told him I was going to be working in during our last conversation. Even if I was still living there, he wouldn't remember my name or who I even was without my rainbow track pants. We would have nothing to talk about, and I would realize my dad was right all along. He was just tall and that is all.

"I am sorry but I am just overly committed right now and not able to hang out. I wish you good luck in the dating world," I texted Mister Superficial.

"Ummmmm ok lol," he texted quickly.

I breathed a sigh of relief.

"That was fairly random so meeting up for lunch and hanging out at the pool is too much for you? Lol," he texted an hour later.

These "lols" were making me furious. I should not have texted back, but I did.

"Yes. Thank you for understanding."

"Well can you at least send me a picture of you in your bathing suit because i am curious to know what i will be missing lol."

When coworker Mike asked how the date went, I showed him the final text and he shook his head and said, "Scum," then looked at me and apologized to me on behalf of all men. "You seem to be getting better at spotting them, the scummy ones," he said, pointing out a silver lining of sorts.

Mike is an older gentleman with white hair and a matching distinguished mustache—think the dude from Monopoly except hairier, stockier, and with a constant twinkle in his eyes. He is the type of guy who is mistaken for Santa Claus by small children.

One cold summer's day when I was wrapped up in my usual giant crochet blanket because the office was always freezing during those months, Mike, as usual, asked aloud if it was hot in here or was it just him. It was always just him. I blame it on the amount of body hair. It keeps him well insulated. This sweet hirsute man then looked at me with a huge smile and asked if I wanted him to throw on a bikini and we could send that picture to "the piece of scum." That image made us both laugh until I had tears coming out of my eyes. When I recovered, we moved on to the more pressing issues of the morning. Mike and I had our own detailed breakfast ritual where he would eat one egg yolk from the two hard boiled eggs I made every morning, and as I cracked and peeled the eggs and we ate, we would discuss what show Mike had fallen asleep to the night before. We never spoke of Mister Superficial again, but to this day, I still wish we took that picture.

Seventeen

Mister Yet Another Wrinkled T-Shirt

Chapel Hill, NC circa 2012

As with most things in life, I have found that I get what I pay for, and OkStupid did not cost a thing. Mister Yet Another Wrinkled T-Shirt was my last OkStupid date. He was 34, played guitar, and didn't have a clue. Before the date, he wanted to speak on the phone to go over a plan. He wanted to call me. This was different. I normally texted people with no pre-date organizational discussion required. The voicemail on my phone says hang up and text me. I work in a call center answering medical information calls for a pharmaceutical company. I spend my entire day on the phone. The last thing I want to do after work is pick up a ringing phone and talk more—I don't care who you are.

I don't tell him any of this, and against every fiber of my being, I tell him, "Sure, call me!" I was thinking at least it would be a short conversation. When he finally called, I suggested Open Eye for a coffee. He launched into a story about a time he went there and received poor customer service, so he didn't want to go back. This was whiney-old-grandpa talk. Who is complaining about customer service in their 30's? This is something you save for conversations in your 60's. This guy was running out of good conversation material fast. I made a mental note to pack both editions of the conversation cards. He then suggested Jesse's, which is another coffee shop. When I told him about a weird experience I had there regarding a sparkling Americano, he dismissed it, "It doesn't sound that bad."

The sparkling Americano was listed as a special, advertised as "disturbingly refreshing." I thought that was odd, but I ordered it anyway. I love an Americano! The barista that made it said no one else had ordered it all day, so he wanted to know if "disturbingly refreshing" was accurate. He checked on me every 15 minutes to see just how disturbingly refreshed I was, which was disturbing. In the end, I conceded to Jesse's. I did enjoy that sparkling Americano (sans check-ins). We had a place and a time, and I thought, "Ok, time to hang up now," but no, he wanted to talk. He wanted to talk about what I did, talk about what he did for a living, talk about his ex-girlfriend ... He had another 30 minutes of stuff to say. I didn't understand why he was launching into all of this. What would we talk about on our actual date? Also, during his 30-minute monologue, I didn't have the heart to tell him that I was sitting in my car in the driveway of my house, in the dark. He had called me on my drive home. I kept thinking the conversation would end at any moment. I was purposefully not contributing but somehow it was moving right along without me.

I stay up late. I always thought the title of my autobiography would be, Vacuuming at Midnight. I had things to do but I didn't want to go into the house and trigger my Cocker Spaniels who must go through a barking fit every time anyone, including myself, enters the house.

"I must go bake a Funfetti cake for Eugene, a coworker who never had one. It's getting kinda late," I said truthfully. Eugene had never experienced the delicious joy of Funfetti and it was important to me to remedy that. I think Mister Wrinkled T-Shirt thought baking a cake was my equivalent of "washing my hair".

"Really? You need to bake a cake, now, at 9 pm?"

"Yes, we can pick-up where we left off tomorrow. I'm looking forward to it!" What I meant by that was, "I'm completely dreading it! Bye."

I was first to arrive for the date and the coffee shop he had championed was already closed. It wasn't even 7pm. I called him and proposed Carrburritos since I was starving.

I hadn't dressed up for the date. After the phone conversation I knew I had no interest in him, so I wore jeans, which I had never done before on any date. I figured he would be in jeans or worse. Why make the effort? Normally I take the time to do my hair, makeup, and nails. The guy normally shows up in jeans and a wrinkled t-shirt. This guy was no exception. For this date, I had put my needs first, for a change. I had come straight from work and had not eaten. I was hangry. We were going to eat some messy Mexican food.

He told me he had stopped off to get a beer before a work meeting he was supposed to attend before our date but had run into a friend and one beer became two and he ended up completely missing the meeting. That was why he was now late to our date. I rolled my eyes, flagrantly, and he didn't seem to notice. I was happy I had not put in the effort. I roll my eyes so much that sometimes I don't even realize I am doing it. When I did it around Mister Ring of Fire, he would burst out laughing.

"Do you realize I just asked you if this place is OK for dinner and you just sighed and rolled your eyes at me?" said Mister Ring of Fire.

I truly did not realize. I needed to be more careful. This behavior is rooted in decision making and how I hate making them. In Religion 101, after I learned some basic stuff about Hasidic Judaism, I realized their belief that since God was speaking directly to their Rabbi, when their Rabbi told them what to do, they were always confident it was the correct decision because it came from God vis-a-vis their Rabbi. Can you imagine being 100% confident in your decisions? This sounded like something I wanted to get in on. I called up my closest Jewish friend, Cara, to discuss possible conversion and she laughed at me. I told her I already had a deep love for and an extensive collection of Klezmer music, Jewish soul music. She dismissed my CD and tape collection as irrelevant.

My introduction to Klezmer started in high school. I was in the pit orchestra for Fiddler on the Roof and that coincided with Itzhak Perlman, my favorite violinist, releasing a Klezmer album. I could not get enough of this beautiful music. I even sought out live performances, and since I couldn't drive yet, my father drove me an hour to go to a Klezmer concert. It only happened once because one Klezmer concert was more than enough for him. He sat there taking it all in and when we were asked to sing along to songs we had never heard before, I could see my dad looking around at the other concert goers. He was at a loss.

"We're the only ones who don't know the words!" he whispered to me. I thought my father would enjoy Klezmer. He was the reason I started playing violin when I was three. Technically, the violin was a ruler attached to a margarine box that I played with a stick, but everyone knows this is the gateway to a full-on, tiny, rented violin. I still remember how exciting that day was when I got to play an actual violin. I now own two violins but haven't played in years. I will be forever grateful to my high school violin teacher who gave me a way out. She was being extremely generous when she said, "Now is the time you either devote your life to the violin or you do something else."

I responded quickly: "I'm ready to do something else."

I skipped to my car after that lesson, feeling completely free and happy to enter college without my violin. Even after years of playing, it always felt foreign to me. Despite my best efforts, I still find myself playing the violin from time to time in my dreams.

My Jewish friend Cara went on to explain why converting would not be a good life decision for me. She knew that I would never subscribe to the ultra-modest dress code for Hasidic women. When it came to my hair and wardrobe, I could never have abided. So, just like that, I was back to a lifetime of eye rolling and questionable decision making.

When my last OkStupid date arrived, he continued to lower my expectations. We ordered our food and when the Carrburritos cashier asked, "Together or separate?" I quickly answered, "Separate!" There was no need to say anything else, but he couldn't help himself.

"If we were together, I would pay for everything. I know we're not together really … This is more like an interview rather than a date. I've had too many first dates lately where I paid and then never got a second date."

Sigh. I just smiled at him and looked away. I hoped the man making my nachos heard and felt bad for me. This was just the beginning of an awkward conversation that lasted exactly an hour and a half.

After he finished eating, he asked, "Is it ok if I smoke since we're outside?"

"Of course!" I said, but I really wanted to yell "Liar!" He never indicated that he was a smoker. This was the second time I had encountered a sneaky smoker. He had just left it off his profile.

As I watched him smoke, I was reminded of my co-worker Bill's words, "You never want to wear Eau de Marlboro, it doesn't suit you." When I was done thinking how wise Bill is, I realized my date was very proudly showing me his AC/DC bottle opener keychain. Oh brother. This seemed like a good stopping point. I didn't even bother breaking out the conversation cards.

"Cool," I said, regarding the chain, before letting us endure an awkward silence.

"Are you ready to get a coffee?" he asked.

"No, it's *Top Chef* night. Every Wednesday my friends and I get together to watch *Top Chef* on Bravo while eating massive amounts of cheese, drinking wine, and just catching up. It's a great way to break up the week and really just an excuse to get together." "Well, enjoy your *Top Chef* night," he said, as if it didn't exist. I smiled at him again, very happy to be headed to see my friends, slurp some wine, pound some cheese, and enjoy my *Top Chef* night. Oh, and there was a special bonus activity: deactivating my OKStupid account.

Eighteen

Mister Faux Manicorn

Durham/Chapel Hill, NC circa 2012

Through eHarm, I had two more dates lined up. The first of two Brian's started off strong, but before meeting for dinner he wanted to have a phone conversation (another phone conversation, sigh), "To discuss where to eat," he said.

Initially, I thought he was thoughtful because he lived in Cary and I in Carrboro—a 40-minute drive away. But why did this warrant a phone conversation and not just another email? I didn't spend too much time thinking about it, which was a mistake. After hopping on the phone, I quickly realized I was in a full-on wife interview. Brian-1 was recently divorced and had two young daughters.

"I was built for marriage and I'm ready to serve a wife." I didn't follow. I had no idea how to take this.

"Well, I would need to speak with your ex-wife to back up these claims," is what I should've said. But he spoke so earnestly. Who was he trying to convince, me or him? Maybe he was just repeating things he had heard at church or in therapy. The real question was what was he going to serve me?

"I like that you have a profession. My last girlfriend didn't. She was just looking for someone to support her. I already have an ex-wife and two kids to support, so I don't need one more person on that list." How romantic!

"Where do you see this relationship going?" Brian-1 said. Our "relationship" up to that point had been online interactions prompted by preformulated eHarm questions. We hadn't even met! I was just hoping we could make it through a dinner, with or without my conversation cards. My bar was set so low at this point, I couldn't even limbo under.

Did he think dinner was the equivalent of a marriage proposal? Maybe he was new at dating, even though he had an ex-wife and ex-girlfriend? Of course, I didn't inquire about any of this. Nor did I offer up that I really didn't want to get married, ever, which in retrospect I probably should have.

As I sat outside on my townhome's deck, where I was living a peaceful life with my two cocker spaniels, I began to check out of the conversation. I had never dated anyone with kids, let alone two, and they were little girls. They would hate me or love me and then his ex-wife would hate me, at least this is how it had always played out in the movies. Then I felt bad for not giving him a chance and not being completely honest with him. I thought I should at least meet him for one date. Maybe he was just nervous?

Even though every fiber of my being wanted to hang up on him, I calmly interrupted him and said maybe we should save something to talk about for when we meet? Which finally brought the conversation around to the original purpose: where to eat. We settled on a place and I was already wishing something would happen to prevent the date from actually occurring.

My magical thinking worked! But, only after I had put my hair up in all those bobby pins, applied makeup and nail stickers, and put on my dress, belt, and cowboy boot uniform. I texted him an hour before the date to see if he had made the reservation and to say that I was looking forward to meeting him (while also praying he was going to punk out on me). He texted back that he sent me an email through eHarm a few minutes ago. Something had come up with his family and he had to cancel. He never once used the word sorry, but the use of the word "family" came through loud and clear, like a slap in the face. He already had a family and had no time "to serve" me.

Why hadn't he called me? It was less than an hour before the date. Certainly, a call or text is less time consuming and more effective than an email through eHarm? Either way, I was totally relieved. No more wasting time on this guy and wondering exactly what he planned on serving me. I had given him a fair chance.

I couldn't let the dressing up go to waste, so I went out with SDH and Crafty and never heard from him again or got that apology. Coward.

This leads me to Brian-2. Although he was 45 minutes late to our first date, he more than made up for it in conversation. He was smart, funny, and cute. Was this my Manicorn? He didn't let me pay for a thing. "I'm from the South and if my grandmother found out I let a girl pay for something on a date, she would roll over in her grave," Brian-2 said.

I guess now is as good a time as any to discuss feminism. I won't spend a lot of time here because even Dolly Parton gets a little uncomfortable when the F word comes up. When she was asked directly by Jad Abumrad in the Dolly Parton's America podcast if she thought of herself as a feminist, she said "No, I do not. I think of myself as a woman in business. I love men." She felt the need to add this statement too: "I do not like extreme things." This answer was surprising but I guess part of Dolly's magic is that she can serve as a model feminist without actually identifying as one. I was called a feminist once, at a fancy dinner with a group of pharmacists in Savannah. My pharmacist friend Monte was next to me at dinner along with some of our former pharmacy classmates. I was seated across from a pharmacist I didn't know and seated next to him was his wife who was also, you guessed it, a pharmacist. He started asking the standard questions. Are you married? Do you have kids? I could see him eyeing my Betsy Johnson submarine sandwich clutch as he asked these questions. Monte and I have been through this line of questioning a million times before, both separately and together, and we smiled and answered "no" to both inquiries—giving no explanations or elaborations. The inevitable pause settled over us, where you try to figure out where else the conversation can go. Movies? Weather? Books?

The waiter was handing out menus to the females first. When the man in front of me finally got his menu, he lowered his reading glasses and said to me directly, "I am assuming you are a feminist, so how does this make you feel?"

No one had ever called me the F word in public. I looked at Monte and smiled and said, "I have the perfect Golden Girls quote as an answer to your question. It's a Blanche quote, specifically, if you're familiar with the Golden Girls?" This would be the only time in my life when I had the perfect answer, and it is all thanks to Natasha.

Natasha did my nails right before the pharmacy trip. While she was carefully painting, she always told me about the Golden Girls episode she had watched that day.

I said, "According to Blanche Devereaux, 'I don't want to be treated as your equal. I want to be treated a lot better than you.' " The man seated across from me smiled and at the end of the meal he walked out next to me, leaning in to ask me where he could get a submarine sandwich purse for his daughters.

Back to Brian-2. So, here's the thing: I always pay for myself, no matter what. If the guy is arrogant, I will pay for him too, just to take him down a notch. It's also a safety issue. I've learned that if you let a man pay, he expects something from you. Although it made me very uncomfortable, I let Brian-2 pay. I couldn't upset grandma, after all. Plus, it made me feel like we were on an "actual" date, like on television. It felt surreal.

Brian-2 had some bad dating experiences that rivaled my own. We bonded quickly. I told him about my conversation cards and he insisted that I bring them on the next date. I didn't have the heart to tell him that versions one and two were already on our date, they were just tucked out of sight in the AstroTurf purse. He asked me if I had any dating successes and I said that I had but with a "Peter Pan type," aka Mister Loner.

"Wait, hold up, he can fly?! I didn't know the competition was that steep. I can't fly!" Brian-2 said.

OMG! He was witty too?! Swoon! We stayed at the restaurant until it was only us and one other table. The staff was cleaning around us. I thanked him for a good date. That was a first. He had dressed up, he had a degree, and was working on his second one. Did I mention he was cute? I was convinced I had finally met my Manicorn.

Our second date was my favorite because we laughed almost the entire time. We went to the Local 506 to hear two bands neither of us knew. I feel like there are two types of people at concerts, those that dance and those that don't. Crafty likes to dance at concerts and in between dancing and trying to get me to dance at a Cat's Cradle concert once, she yelled, "Hey, you need to put in your profile that you do not dance at concerts!" She had a point. I am forever grateful that she pointed this out because she is right, there is nothing that ruins a concert faster than someone trying to make me dance.

Brian-2 got a drink and sat down with me. Perfect. The first band was awesome. The second played what sounded like the same song over and over again. When I told him how much I had liked the first band, as we were enduring the second band, he politely excused himself. I thought he was getting another drink or powdering his nose, but he came back with a copy of the first band's CD for both him and myself. He was thoughtful too! It was almost too much for me to handle. I was living my version of the Sex and the City episode when Carrie is dating Baryshnikov and she has to tell him it is too much romance and that she is an American and he has to turn it down a notch.

One thoughtful gesture, on top of him dressing up and making me laugh, was all I needed to be swept off my feet. I had thought I was unsweepawayable! My friend Shannon used this word when she was talking about her now husband, specifically about how he had intended on proposing to her in a hot air balloon in Europe. All he wanted to do was sweep her off her feet. There was a language issue and, long story short, she was proposed to on land and he was upset. She comforted him: "Thank God! What would we have done for the rest of the time trapped in that tiny balloon basket with a stranger?" She was already in love with him, I could see it, and when I asked her directly after a night of cocktails if she thought he was the one she would marry, she looked at me with a huge smile on her face and said "oh, I would love to marry him!" A hot air balloon was not going to change anything.

When they first started dating, I was around them for a week at the Sundance Film Festival. I was the stranger in their hot air balloon. It was obvious to me they were in their own little world, complete with non-stop giggling. He just had to make her laugh; no hot air required. She had guilt for feeling that way about the planned balloon proposal but concluded the story by identifying as unsweepawayable. At the time, I could not have identified more with this made-up word.

The Faux Manicorn and I had gone on four dates and I was beginning to think that he could be the guy that I slip into domestic bliss with. The fact that he was considering a job in Ohio didn't faze me. I could move, which is something I'd never considered before. It would mean breaking one of Angry Dave's cardinal rules. "You don't move for the D," Angry Dave always said. I was sure Angry Dave would make an exception for me in this particular case.

I was excitedly discussing Faux Manicorn with Carmen, one of my oldest and dearest friends, and she looked at my four-year-old goddaughter, her daughter, and said, "Well, I guess we're moving to Ohio!" She was joking, but this is when I realized that I needed to slow things down. A move was not just going to impact me, and I needed to be absolutely sure about this dude. The glorious byproduct of me being single for so long has been that I have been able to have and maintain incredibly strong friendships with people who have turned out to be the lights of my life. There was an article in *The Wall Street Journal* about how the only thing in life that is actually priceless is art. I politely disagree, what is truly priceless are friendships. Think about it. They can't be bought.

If there is one thing I have eventually learned from conversations with friends about dating, it is to heed red flags. I have had many conversations with Angry Dave where he frantically waves his arm in my face while shouting repeatedly, "Red flag!" after I casually mention something in passing about a romantic interest. I needed to take a closer look at Mister Faux Manicorn and see him through the eyes of Angry Dave.

I used to blow right through red flags, frantically waving them out of my way like flies at a cookout trying to get in the way of me and my hot dog. Angry Dave has yelled at me about how no one takes his advice when it comes to relationships, but he is always right. He tried to warn me about Mister Ghost and I didn't listen. Now, at the mention of Mister Ghost's name Angry Dave just says, "Fuuuck him." Mister Ghost could discover that the cure for cancer was actually on one of Pluto's moons and Angry Dave would say "fuck that guy".

I had figured out that maybe I didn't need to go down another dark path lined with red flags. Angry Dave was like my GPS popping up in the middle of the route, letting me know that I can't see it yet, but there is an accident ahead. If I tap the button, I can be rerouted around it and save some time. Thank God for that button and for Angry Dave.

When I would ask Brian-2 what he did the night before, the answer always involved a strip club and him being there alone. I didn't know what to ask without sounding like I was judging him, so I decided to just be honest and say that I had never been to a strip club. I had hoped he would then explain why he was always there. He didn't. I could envision Angry Dave furiously hoisting a red flag in my face for this one.

"Well, I am not taking you to this strip club," Brian-2 said. As it turned out, it sounded like he spent a fair amount of time there. He proudly stated that he knew all of the strippers by their real names and their real problems. He said he knew who was trying to finish school, who was struggling in math class, and who was saving up for what. He spoke about the people who worked at the strip club as if they were his friends. Maybe they all were? After telling me all about his friends, he would also make it very clear I could never go there. It was his place.

Angry Dave would have been lost in a tornado of red flags at this point.

Brian-2 told me one strip club story, prefacing it by saying he should probably not tell me the story. His best friend was dating a stripper. When they picked her up from the airport, the ride took a sudden, sexually explicit turn. He described when she started masturbating in the backseat of the car, including way too many details that I won't repeat. He and his friend both just watched in the rearview mirror.

Another time, he described going to Cracker Barrel with his father and no stripper. He had the meatloaf and was so full afterwards he passed out.

"The waitress could have put a ketchup bottle up my butt and I would not have woken up," he said. People have described how tired they felt after a meal in a variety of different ways, but this was a new one. I have never been that tired. Woah.

These rambling stories left me speechless and uncomfortable. I tried to change the subject multiple times. As you already know, I had worked at an HIV and AIDS hotline for teens during high school and college, and had taught sex ed a couple times to middle school students. I have no problem talking about sex, but this guy was making me blush.

Shortly after the ketchup-butt date, I went out of town for my birthday on a long weekend excursion to New York City. After being with close friends and family and discussing Faux Manicorn and his explicit red flags, it became clear that he wasn't my Manicorn. I didn't want a man in my life that enjoyed telling me stories that made me uncomfortable and spent most nights in a strip club without me. Although he was the closest I had ever come to my Manicorn, this guy was a fake.

Due to Hurricane Sandy, SDH and I were delayed coming home from New York for hours. So, after a few airport Basil Bellinis, I made up my mind to end it via text with my usual line. He agreed that I probably wasn't the girl for him and also wished me a safe trip home. That night we made it out of New York on the very last plane before they closed the airport. I took this as a sign my luck was finally changing, but what did I know? I had a hundred dollars' worth of Basil Bellinis in me.

When I got home and sobered up, I wondered if I had made the right decision. While flipping through *W Magazine* I spotted a black and white picture of an older, slim man in a tuxedo with one hand in his pocket. He wore a metal unicorn mask complete with a flowing, curly mane. It was Billy Baldwin (not that one), an interior designer, arriving at Truman Capote's Black and White Ball at the Plaza Hotel in New York in 1966. There was an elegant, real live Manicorn just out there walking around!? I was stunned. I could not take my eyes off him. I looked at the image for several minutes, taking it all in. This was my sign. My Manicorn exists and he is still out there. With tears in my eyes, I cut him out and put him front and center on my altar … errr, fridge. There is nothing more depressing to me than having a naked refrigerator. Mine is covered with pictures, magnets, quotes, coupons, small dry-erase boards, invitations, fortunes, and thank you cards.

I was too young to remember who it was who first told me to make a wish at 11:11 or 2:22 or … you get the idea. It was presented to me like a fact or wish-loophole. Ever since, I've made a wish when all the digital digits are unanimous. I get all excited and silently wish for whatever it is until the magic is over at 2:23. I don't tell anyone what I wish for and move on with my life, with an extra bit of hopefulness.

Circa 2013, after I had pinky sworn away all further communication with Mister Loner, my wishing sounded something like, "Please let the love of my life show up!" It was time for my Manicorn.

Nineteen

Lisa Loeb, Beastie Boys, and My Manicorn

Raleigh, NC Circa 2014

I am constantly on the lookout for signs. Lisa Loeb and one particular Beastie Boys song have provided two huge flashing signs on the highway of my life. In 2006, Lisa Loeb was looking for love on the E! television network. Her show "#1 Single" lasted only one season. One of my friends and coworkers at the time, Amber, had seen the reality show and mentioned to me that Loeb's attitude towards dating reminded her of my own and that I should check it out. I was instantly hooked.

Loeb was a Carrie Bradshaw in glasses and she was looking for her Jewish Manicorn. I could relate and, of course, became way too emotionally invested. In the end, Loeb shared a kiss with a male friend. That is where she remained, frozen in my head, until, years later, when I read in one of my magazines that she had had her second child. Suddenly, Loeb was back in my life.

I quickly Googled her husband, only to find out it wasn't the man she kissed when the show was canceled. Her new man worked for Conan O'Brien and after she guested on "Late Night with Conan O'Brien," they had talked and he courted her. Apparently, he found her cute and then there was something about a fluffernutter sandwich which led to their marriage.

I, too, love a fluffernutter! This obvious sign leapt off the glossy pages and gave me a tremendous amount of hope—when I needed it the most. The online dating hamster wheel was really taking a toll on my psyche. I was exhausted with nothing to show for it except all these dating stories. Around this time, I was driving home from work in sleet and darkness, thinking about quitting online dating altogether. I would be fine. I alone am enough …

Right?! I had (still do) great friends, two loveable dogs, and a satisfying career surrounded by coworkers I also count as friends. Why was I putting myself through this? If I was meant to meet someone, then I would. My favorite saying is that one about God laughing Her ass off when you make plans.

While switching between five push-button satellite stations on the dash, trying to convince myself, I received a sign. On "Lithium," the 1990s grunge and alternative rock station, "Sure Shot" by the Beastie Boys was playing. Alone in my car, I could not have been smiling any wider. There I was trying to make a plan, and God was laughing, singing along to the Beastie Boys, at me.

The other four stations in my rotation were *Sirius XMU*, the indie pop, rock, and unsigned artist station; the *80s on 8* and *90s on 9* stations, respectively; and last but not least, the *Siriusly Sinatra* station, which was only played in my house when cooking or when guests come over. Turns out the universe speaks to me through the Beastie Boys.

It was actually the second time this song had come on at the exact moment I needed to hear it. The first time occurred early one morning in South Carolina while I was getting my Charleston house ready to sell. I had decided to abandon my life in retail pharmacy in favor of trying my hand at the medical information business back where I had gone to high school and college and where my parents were still living. I was making my millionth Lowes run and thinking about how overwhelming the whole move had become and that I couldn't do it anymore. I was seriously considering keeping the house and continuing to live with my sister and all the extra people that I had allowed to come to live with us. The moment I realized things had gone too far came during a phone call with Monte. "I just really need to get my own place," I said. Monte had to gently remind me that it was my house—I owned it. Somehow, I had completely lost sight of that.

How did that happen? Well, originally it was only my sister and I in the house with one extra bedroom. Then, whenever someone had broken up with their boyfriend and needed a place to go, they came and stayed with us. If a pharmacy intern needed a place to live while on rotations, then they would live with us. We always had people visiting from out of state because we were close to the beach and downtown Charleston. Then my sister's boyfriend moved in, along with his dog Jack, the Jack Russell Terrier. Before I knew it, I was locking myself in my room on the main floor because my kitchen and living room were full of people eating their food with their guests and watching tv shows I didn't watch. It was loud and uncomfortable and I was so stressed out I had forgotten that I was the one who allowed it all to happen.

I needed to escape. But, for a while I thought I could allow it to continue without me. I let my sister Katie live in the house with the people she wanted to live with. That didn't last long, though, because I was never meant to be a landlady. I am not good at asking people for money they owe me or fixing things.

As hard as it was, I had to tell Katie that I was selling the house that she had called home for three years. Things only became more difficult when I hired a realtor who told me all the things that needed to be fixed before I could sell it. I was on a first name basis with many people who worked at Lowes and I was driving back and forth between North and South Carolina every weekend. I would get off work at my new job in North Carolina on a Friday and then drive five hours to South Carolina, wake up early on Saturday and head to Lowe's. It was on one of these early morning Lowe's runs when I began thinking, "I cannot do this anymore!" The moment I had that thought, the Beastie Boys came on, singing directly to me:

" … Because you can't, you won't, and you don't stop!" I turned the music all the way up.

I fixed up my Charleston house, sold it right before the housing market crashed, and started my new life in North Carolina, for the second time since I was 13. So, when I heard the Beastie Boys sign for the second time, I decided not to give up on dating. I would find love, just like Lisa Loeb, because I can't, I won't, and I don't stop.

Those Beastie Boys lyrics are now permanently tattooed on my left shoulder in typewriter font. I can't tell you how many women, most of them drunk while we wait in line for the powder room, have moved my tank aside so they can read ALL the lyrics out loud and then just start singing the song because apparently everyone knows and loves the Beastie Boys.

The ironic thing is that I didn't meet my Manicorn online. I met him on a Saturday night at an Irish Pub after Happily-Ever-After Drag Bingo. It was February and I had convinced my friend Weiderman (Shannon) to come with me. It was a great time even though there were no cocktails involved. After, we went to meet her husband who was still out with people from their yoga studio. When we met up with the yoga crew, it was clear they had been drinking for a while, so I planned on having one drink before heading home. I was themed for the drag bingo, so in addition to my hair being twisted up in a million colored bobby pins, I had on a sweater with giant sequined red lips sewn on the front, and a black wool cape on as my coat. In other words, not at all what I would normally wear out, especially on a date. I ordered a vodka and soda and remained standing, ready to leave.

I have known Weiderman and her husband George for years, but I didn't know anyone else in the group. George introduced me as an artist to the Manicorn. I may have underestimated how drunk they all were. I started to laugh and corrected George. I am not an artist, but, in fact, had gone to pharmacy school with George's wife and was now working with her. The only art I produce is paint by number. The Manicorn started laughing and said, "Paint by number?" I told him that I enjoy it so much that I had thrown a paint-by-number party where we just sat around and painted while drinking out of the party pump.

The party pump is a giant plastic container that holds almost 50 Cosmopolitans. You can pump at will. It was not classy, but super convenient and always a hit. I called the party "Pump and Paint." He looked at me and said, "I want to come to one of your parties." It turned out he was an actual artist, a painter of abstract art, in his spare time.

We were next to the band, so it was hard to hear, but he kept asking if I was married and if I had kids. I would answer and then he would ask the same question. I thought, "Man, he is wasted." Instead, I told him that I really wished I could hear him better. He just looked at me and smiled. He had this calm energy, sitting there with two hands wrapped around a beer, looking at me.

The first thing I notice about someone is their eyes. His eyes always met mine and they were smiling too. They were not blue as my mother's psychic friend predicted, but brown, and he was a happy drunk, good for him! When I was done with my drink and started to go, he stood up, grabbed my hand and asked for my email address. This startled me. Email address? This was a first. When I told him my address, he muttered under his breath, "I'm never going to remember that," and sat back down. He released my hand, and, still looking me in the eyes, asked how he could get in contact with me. As I put on my cape, I said, "George. He knows everything about me. Just ask George." I left feeling confident I would never hear from him again.

Of course, I did hear from him, and when I left Pilates class on Monday night, I had several texts. The first was from Weiderman and it said the Manicorn contacted George and George gave out my number and she hopes that is ok. I told her yes but it's too late for an "ok" because he was already texting me.

As I arrived late to our first date in Durham, I started out with: "I'm saving up for a helicopter because the traffic is so bad." He looked at me and without skipping a beat said, "Where are you going to park this helicopter?" No one ever asked me that, so I smiled and replied, "UNC Hospital is close to me and has helicopters, so maybe I can park it there?"

"Probably not," he said, laughing. He talked to me like he knew me. I felt like I knew him too. No conversation cards, no awkward questions or silences, it was easy to jump in and start talking about anything and everything.

The one thing that kept distracting me was his ears. They are messed up in a way that I can't really explain. It's like someone turned them inside out and they stayed that way. I learn later they are a remnant of his wrestling career and they are known as "cauliflower ears." He is proud of his ears. He gets respect from strangers because of his ears.

We continued to talk and were in our own world until we realized there wasn't a bathroom in the joint. They had closed one side of the restaurant and we were in a side area completely alone. I abruptly ended the date by telling him I was going to Thomas' house. I had planned on going to check on him since it was the anniversary of his father's death and he lived close by the restaurant, so I could use his bathroom while I was there. That is how we ended our first date—me going to my good friend's house and the future Mister Manicorn thinking that I am seeing another guy and that I just left our date to spend time with him.

On our second date, I went to Raleigh where the Manicorn lives. It's about 45 minutes from where I was living in Carrboro, so I was late to arrive, again, and I wasn't sure where to find parking.

I do not possess a sense of direction—at all—and as a result, I am constantly lost. It doesn't matter if I have been there before, even several times before, I will get lost. I parked in a parking garage and took a picture of the street name hoping that I would be able to find my way back as I ran to the restaurant. It was February and cold, so at the end of the date he asked if he could take me to my car. I agreed and confidently told him the name of the street the parking garage was on. Little did I know there were three parking garages on that same street. He took me through all three and my car was literally on the very last level of the third garage. I could not stop apologizing, but he was so calm and patient, it was unbelievable. It was ridiculous to be riding up and down parking garages looking for my car, and after a little while he started asking me if I was sure what my car looked like. He was not mad and was actually joking with me about it. Then he said the thing that made me totally relax and start to love him, "This is funny." Music to my ears! I was so glad that was his take on the situation and he was not annoyed or mad—I thought it was funny too. I was so relieved. I had thought maybe he was going to yell at me or lecture me or just get fed up and leave me to find my car on foot, by myself.

The Manicorn was a pre-K teacher, which I credit with giving him seemingly endless patience. I never knew I would find this quality so attractive in someone. People used to ask what my type was, and I always thought they were referring to what I found physically attractive, and I would answer tall with light eyes. Turns out my type is someone full of patience, thoughtfulness, and humor. I tell him all the time he is the nicest person I've ever met. He really is. To him, this is not a compliment. He will always respond, "I am not that nice." I told him early on that the number one quality I value in a partner is thoughtfulness. After a few days, he told me he had been thinking about this and he didn't think he was thoughtful enough for me. He even asked his mom about his level of thoughtfulness.

He is not taller than me. He has what he refers to as his "champ stamp," which is exactly what you think it is: a tattoo on his lower middle back. It is an Adinkra symbol meaning strength. He does not have blue eyes—let alone light eyes—and has inside out ears. No one is more surprised than me that this would be exactly my type. The Manicorn comes with the added benefit of being packaged in a body that shows the benefits and discipline of working out almost every day of his life. He is constantly being asked what he does to work out, and, with a straight face, he says: yoga. People think he is joking, but to be fair, he is a yoga instructor, who just happens to also lift weights in a hot yoga studio that also provides circuit training classes.

On our third date, I met him right after work at a pizza place in between where we both lived. It was a Friday night, so I was tired and dressed in what I wore to work: a simple, black, short, puffy-sleeved sweater dress and cowboy boots. I was so tired that I had not done my hair that morning. It was down and it had been dried and styled by having my car windows fully open. All I wanted to do was hang out with my Manicorn, so I wasn't even thinking about my hair, makeup, and nails being perfect. It was so freeing.

I felt so calm when I was with him, like G-Love and Special Sauce were whispering in my ear the whole time. We sat there laughing and talking while eating our pizza and drinking wine. There came a moment where he reached over and picked a piece of hair off my black dress. I noticed him really looking at me, smiling. I got nervous and said, "What?"

"You look great, " he said to me for the first time. I had never had someone say that to me so earnestly before. I didn't know what to say. I didn't feel like I looked great at all, but all I could do was smile. He was allowing me to be completely myself and, on top of that, he complimented me for it. I was in such foreign territory, I had no words.

He walked me to my car after dinner and as we were standing by my car saying goodnight, he tried to kiss me. I say tried because I turned my head and he spun around and played it off. It was just a bad habit, a knee-jerk reaction to the dreaded sneak-attack kiss, only this time I felt terrible. I should have kissed him. To this day I still relive it, and we have never talked about it.

I realized that all this time these "sneak-attack kisses" were normal. There was nothing sneaky about them. I was just avoiding them and it became a habit. We ended up having our first kiss at my house, on my vintage yellow pleather couch, on our fourth date. We were laughing about how I was going to a Bruce Springsteen concert and didn't know any of his songs. The last thing Manicorn said to me as he was moving closer was, "I want to see Bruce Springsteen too," and then he kissed me. It was perfect.

Without traffic, we lived 45 minutes apart. On Friday nights, I would load up my car with the two dogs and all their necessities, all the food and snacks I felt like we needed to get through the weekend (enough for a week), my magazines, a box of wine, etc. Produx does not travel light!

On my third trip from the car to his apartment, the Manicorn was looking at me with an open mouth. All I could say was, "I can't do less than this." This is Produx. He smiled and noticed the bag of Oreos on the top of one of the food bags, "You brought Oreos?!" I would learn later it was his favorite cookie.

It was during one of these first Friday nights that the box of wine broke. It hadn't happened to me before (or since). We had to put the wine in any container we could find because it just kept coming. We were drinking and laughing and waiting for a whole chicken to cook. I asked my Manicorn what his next tattoo would be and he didn't hesitate, "The number 15." I was ready with follow up questions like, "What does the 15 stand for and why is it a significant number for you?" He just looked at me and said, "It's the date we met."

I have never been more shocked in my life. The next day I checked my calendar because I had no idea what that date actually was. Of course, he was right. He has the roman numeral 15 on his forearm in a floating banner at the end of some beautiful flowers.

The best way I can describe our relationship is that I feel like I am in a never-ending romantic comedy. On our fifth date, I wanted to be honest with him about our future, in case he felt like he was built to serve his wife. I came right out and told him, while we were sitting at our local secret bar, that if he wanted to get married and have kids, then I wasn't the girl for him. This is how I started the date and it was the first time I said it on a date. Ever. He paused and smiled and stuck out his pinky and we pinky swore. I have our pinky swear tattooed to me now, along with the floating banner with the roman numeral 15. Daniel, the tattoo artist in New York City, is the one that made it such a beautiful and interesting piece. I asked for two generic hands and a pinky promise. He said we needed to know one was a female hand and one was a male hand.

I still don't want marriage and kids, but now it has become more about not wanting anything to bring our romantic comedy to an end or turn it into some melodrama or cheesy action-adventure movie. I am too old to be the one pulling my kids out of the police paddy wagon in my robe. Nope. Not interested.

When I met the Manicorn, my ship dropped anchor. I got a tattoo in red ink of an anchor with a heart on top, seamlessly attached to an infinity sign. It's the most optimistic tattoo I have. After a couple weeks of dating Mister Manicorn, I would just start crying on the way to work thinking about my life. I was so happy. It would catch me off guard and it was almost always triggered by a song. At that time, there was a song that was playing regularly on Sirius XMU called "Thunder Clatter" by Wild Cub, and if that came on, I would end up sobbing. The lyrics spoke directly to my heart: the protagonist of the song finds the love of his life in the dead of winter. Finally, I was able to identify with happy love songs and now they all made me cry. Barf, I know.

He is everything I was looking for, my Manicorn. If it meant that I had to go through all this again, even the stuff I didn't tell you about, just to end up with him, I would choose to go through it all again. Every single fucking second. The puking, endless eye rolling, billions of sighs, conversation card fails, pounds and pounds of wasted lip gloss, the not so artful dodging of sneak-attack kisses, wife interviews, all the times I picked C, gallons of vodka, and an egg saturated beard—he's worth it all.

Twenty

Coda

"Because Prince Charming Isn't Coming …" That was the subject line from an email about financial planning that landed in my inbox in the middle of my online dating days, thanks to my subscription to *BUST* magazine. *BUST* is not what you're thinking. In its own words, it's a "women's lifestyle magazine that is unique in its ability to connect with bright, cutting-edge, influential young women". I call it an indie feminist magazine that speaks directly to my taste in books, music, fashion, recipes, and crafts. SDH had gifted me a subscription a million years ago and I was hooked.

Yes, I still get magazines. Several in fact, even *Garden and Gun*. I had a telemarketer call me one day and explain that if I completed a survey, I would get a subscription to my favorite magazine. I politely declined his offer, stating that I already get all my favorite magazines. The telemarketer laughed and started naming magazines and asking me if I already got them. I played along for a while. He thought I was kidding and kept laughing when I told him I was already getting all the magazines he was naming. Then I listed off the rest of the magazines I was already getting. When he realized I was serious, he stopped and asked me, in all seriousness, "Why are you getting all these magazines?" That is how I ended up telling a stranger about my love of magazines.

My favorite thing to do on a Sunday morning is read a magazine backwards while drinking a homemade Americano with heavy cream. The best! "I don't remember when I started reading them backwards," I answered. "I think I started because the first part is mostly ads. I just want to jump in, and when I'm done reading everything, the mindless ads are a nice way to wind down." The telemarketer replied "Ahh, that makes sense." Suddenly, we were having an intense conversation about what makes us the happiest.

"If I'm having a bad day, can I call you to chat and check-in?" the telemarketer asked.

"Sure!" I said. He called a bunch soon after and it quickly got to be too much. As much as it pained me, I stopped picking up. He was cutting into my precious magazine reading time.

Anyway, I was not surprised when I found the source behind the unusually frank subject line, but it had certainly gotten my attention. Being a single woman in my 30's, the notion of Prince Charming came up more than I thought it should. (Damn you, Disney)! For a while I felt like I was patiently awaiting him. When he wasn't showing, I began to freak out and question his very existence. Maybe my Prince wasn't charming and I had already met him? Are only certain people allotted a Prince Charming and I didn't make the cut? There must be a percentage of Prince Charming's that can't ride a horse or drive a car? At one point, I thought My Prince Charming must be bedridden, a shut-in, or perhaps already dead. That has got to happen right? I don't mean that my Prince Charming was someone to ride into my life and rescue me. I dreamed of him as this simple man that would take me by the hand and lead me to domestic bliss. Deep down I hoped he existed. I ended countless journal entries with some sort of variation on the thought, or wish, that I was ready for my *simple kind of life*. On bad days, I would plead, "Where the HELL was my simple kind of life, the one alluded to by Gwen Stefani in the "No Doubt" song of the same name?!"

Years were going by and I watched the bulk of my friends get married and start having kids and then more kids. Meanwhile, I had never been in a relationship that lasted even close to a year, at least consecutive years. It took me a while to realize that the simple kind of life I was pining for was the opposite of simple to achieve. I don't think anyone with a marriage or a marriage and kids would ever describe their life as simple either. Eventually, I had a front row seat to the crumbling of many friends' simple kind of lives.

Planning and paying for a wedding? Having a child in my 40's? This is the stuff of my nightmares. I met my Manicorn when I was 35. I was exhausted by the time I finally found him, so no, I do not want marriage and kids. It's funny to think back to when my parents had me tested to see if I had a learning disability. For my "specific problems" I was accommodated with extra time on every test for the duration of my education. I didn't realize then that this need for extra time would carry over to my romantic life as well.

At the time I received the financial planning email from *BUST*, I was still waiting and wondering where the hell Prince Charming was with my motherfucking simple kind of life. I had not anticipated the message that he wasn't coming anytime soon to arrive in an email to my yahoo account. It totally shook me up (this was before people were just "shook")! It felt personal. So much so that the day I received the email, I cried twice while thinking about it—at work. Mike reluctantly asked me what was the matter.

He had already made me feel better by telling me that there is no crying in baseball but there is crying in our call center warehouse job. The last thing I wanted to say was that I was crying about a financial planning email blast that involved Prince Charming, but I did. Instead of laughing at me, he thoughtfully paused, munched a mini carrot, looked me in the eyes and said, "He is just on a delay." I accepted his answer not only because Mike is the smartest person I know, but because of my belief in the *perfect*.

There was a time I was so stressed out that I forgot to look at my *perfect* wrist tattoo. I had a townhome in Carrboro, North Carolina, that I was renting out to tenants when Mister Manicorn and I first started living together. An attic pipe had frozen and burst, which somehow proceeded to trigger the entire sprinkler system, causing thousands of gallons of water to soak all four floors, including all the tenant's belongings. It was a full-on disaster. We later found out it was an old issue with the pipes and the builder had long since gone out of business.

The fire chief had called me at work to let me know there was water pouring out of the second-story windows. They had to break down the front door to get inside because they didn't know if anyone was in the house.

I pictured that scene from the animated *Alice in Wonderland* where she cries so much as giant Alice that everything begins to float on her tears, including Alice, who, by the time her tears had turned into a flood, had drunk that potion, and shrunk.

When I arrived with my father to see for myself, there was still water dripping down every wall. The walls were crying. After the man with the water damage restoration company finished showing us all the damage, it was so shocking that my dad asked, "Are you not shocked because you see this all the time?" The man just looked at my dad with no emotion and said, "Oh, this is clean water, this is no problem. We just have to dry this place out. If it were sewage water, we'd have real problems."

I immediately thanked him for sharing that. It gave me perspective. Alice was the right size again. It made my attitude of gratitude kick in and I challenged myself to think of two other things I was grateful for, to keep from crying. It could always be worse.

Next came several months of me trying to meet the needs of the contractors, the insurance company, the bank, the renter, and the property management company. It was a lot to juggle along with my full-time job. Then I was at a yoga class one night, trying to relax in the dark, surrounded by battery-operated candles while attempting to get into a seated-spine twist, when I caught a glimpse of my wrist in the artificial light. I saw the "perfect ... " for the first time in a while and burst out laughing.

It was like Dorothy and those ruby slippers. I had the power the entire time. Everything was going to be fine because everything is *perfect*, exactly the way it should be.

This ideal that my wrist tattoo represents does not resonate with everyone. I have friends who look like they want to punch me when I tell them that whatever horrible news they just told me is happening for a reason and it is all "perfect." To each her own coping mechanism.

I know now that I should not have been waiting for Prince Charming or my Manicorn because they were going to show up once I realized that I didn't really need them to show up. I could save myself—thank you very much. I was privileged to be able to create my own life based on what makes me happy and, without realizing it, I had done it all on my own. I created my version of the simple kind of life.

When I finally realized this, there was a distinct shift in my journal entries. I no longer begged for my simple kind of life. I expressed my gratitude for everything on those sacred pages. No matter what happened, good or bad, I ended every entry with a thank you. No more anger, no more sadness, no more pleading, no more questioning, just a thank you for everything. Who am I thanking, exactly? The universe? God? Everyone I've ever known? Myself? The mirror in the sky from the Landslide song? Truthfully, whoever is listening is welcome to my gratitude.

Recently, my Manicorn was away for the weekend with his best friends. I am not one to get up early. I love to sleep as late as possible. I swap shifts with all my coworkers so that I can have the later shifts. Anyway, my Manicorn called to see how my weekend was going and he said, "You're probably having the best time ever, sleeping in with no one bothering you." Before I could answer, he said, "You know why I wake you up so early? Because being with you is like Christmas morning. I'm so excited that I want to wake you up as early as possible." I was so overwhelmed by him, I just started to cry. It is the best thing I have ever heard in my life and everything I ever wanted. We spent the rest of the phone call with me crying and him laughing at me for crying.

Once I worked with a pharmacy technician named Brenden who, after I asked him what his philosophy on life was, told me that he just wished there was more magic. That was it. At the time, I thought this was the stupidest thing I had ever heard. Magic? I didn't get it. When we would work together in the pharmacy and the satellite would go out and there was no music or ads playing, I would immediately point out to him that it was so nice to have silence for a while. One time, I wasn't sure if he had heard me. Then after a while he said, "It took me so long to process what you were saying because there was still music playing in my head." Strange Bird—that's what I called him in the contacts in my phone.

Eventually, I realized that magic could mean a moment or something that felt magical and special, and when I finally started to notice these moments, I too wanted more. Somehow, the Manicorn has a seemingly endless supply of magic. But don't get me wrong, I don't want to jinx our relationship by putting up a happily-ever-after banner. Although I am enjoying the magic of our domestic bliss, I don't ever want to take it for granted or assume it will somehow last forever.

Ira Glass said something very candid during a This American Life episode; it felt like a confession. It was something about him feeling like he had to prove himself to his wife every day, followed by this nervous laugh. Ira just shared his truth! You can feel it when you are presented with the truth. I imagined my middle school English teacher shining a light on it and saying, here it is! I remember this particular middle school lecture on feeling the truth because I actually felt it. I had not been paying attention, and in an effort to get and keep the attention of middle schoolers, the teacher would often resort to a by-any-means-necessary tactic. Bruce, (at Quaker school you call your teachers by their first name), delivered a dramatic monologue while standing very close to me, looking me straight in the eye. At the end, he threw his body around my legs. In the process of grabbing my legs, he pulled a little too hard and he pulled me off my stool and my butt hit the floor. It was painful, mortifying, and I can still smell the moment because he was a smoker who had chili for lunch.

From that day forward, I paid attention to every single word that came out of his mouth. I never wanted that to happen again. He taught me so many things, when I finally started to listen. He was so passionate and had such a love for literature and the English language. He is responsible for my love of reading. Somehow, he had transferred it to me, perhaps during the moment my butt hit the floor.

I like when people are honest about how they exist in their relationships. But it worried me that if Ira, who in my mind seemed pretty perfect on my radio every week, was having to prove himself every day, then I really had my work cut out for me. It sounded exhausting. When I found out he was getting a divorce, somewhere in early 2017, my first thought was, well, maybe, hopefully he can finally rest now. Lucky bastard.

Last year, Mister Ring of Fire asked me what I had learned since turning 40. It had been a whole month since my birthday. He asked me during the endless previews before the movie we went to see with his sister and twin brother. I was caught off guard by his question, so I quickly responded that I would have to get back to him with my answer. After much thought, I texted an answer: *No one really knows what they are doing. The only thing of value is friendships. Lastly, it has become clear to me that the only thing I have been working towards is ending my day with a scented candle burning, ensconced in my favorite spot—the couch with the Manicorn and our dogs—eating, talking, laughing, and watching TV with a glass of wine or cup of tea in my hand.* Domestic Freakin' Bliss. I had arrived and it was even cozier than I'd thought.

Several years after I got the *perfect* tattoo, I decided to get "ovaries before brovaries" tattooed on my back. It was done by a beautiful pixie of a tattoo artist, Meghan, that I regularly see in Chapel Hill with Mister Manicorn for our anniversary tattoos. I would not be surprised if she has a subscription to BUST magazine too.

Manicorn and I have our own tradition of getting tattoos to celebrate the day we met. We don't get the same tattoo; just tattoos on the same day by Meghan. Meghan looked at "ovaries before brovaries," smiled, and gave me the highest praise I have ever received from a tattoo artist, "Mary Gulla, I just love your shit!"

When we came back the next year, she had put the stencil of the tattoo on her window for all to see. It was during one of these anniversary tattoo trips that I wanted to finally get my Manicorn tattoo. I wanted the head of a unicorn on the body of a man in a tuxedo. I wanted to make it similar to the image of the original Manicorn from *W Magazine*. What Meghan came up with was so perfect that we, and the lady that works the front desk, could not stop giggling. As she was setting up to ink me, Megan asked about the significance of this black-tie unicorn. I ended my explanation by pointing to the real life Manicorn and the giggling started all over again. My Manicorn shaves his head bald, so his permanently flowing mane in the tattoo is particularly funny. The Manicorn is used to it.

In addition to creating the perfect Manicorn tattoo, Meghan also came up with the perfect placement: my upper-middle back, "so his unicorn head pokes out of every tank top you wear." When I look in the mirror at my back, there he is, peeking out with his rainbow horn and flowing mane. It makes me smile every time.

Things came full circle earlier in 2020, before COVID, with Lisa Loeb. I finally got to see her perform in person as the headliner at the Snowball musical showcase in Party City. It was magic! There she was on stage in a little black short sleeved dress with black tights and black shoes, with her guitar and iconic glasses. She was adorable, complete with charming banter and a pink guitar strap. When she sang "Stay", high-school-me was in heaven. She sang the song I had heard a million times and knew all the words to, but I didn't sing along because I just wanted to hear her. I was mesmerized for her entire set. I didn't move or want it to end. Before and after "Stay", she sang a bunch of songs I had never heard, but it didn't matter, I was sharing the same air as Lisa Loeb. As she left the stage, I clapped like the maniac Lisa Loeb groupie I am and silently thanked her as she left the stage.

Well, I think the perfect way to end our time together is with a Mike quote: "It wasn't pretty, but it worked. So far, it's the story of my life." I know you probably have had your own online dating experiences and I want to hear them. If you're just starting out, hit me up too! Please find me on social media if you want to share your dating stories.

Twenty-One

Tunes

"Sure Shot"	Beastie Boys
"Two Weeks"	Grizzly Bear
"Changed the Locks"	Lucinda Williams
"Tire Swing"	Kimya Dawson
"Edit the Sad Parts"	Modest Mouse
"Run Devil, Run"	Jenny Lewis and the Watson Twins
"Naked Eye"	Luscious Jackson
"Tati un Mama Tants"	Itzhak Pearlman and The Andy Statman Klezmer Orchestra
"Help me Rhonda"	The Beach Boys
"Thunder Clatter"	Wild Cub
"Abra Cadaver"	The Hives
"Ring of Fire"	Johnny Cash
"Best of Friends"	Palma Violets
"Nodding Off"	Wavves, featuring Best Coast
"Simple Kind of Life"	No Doubt
"Stay"	Lisa Loeb
"Pull the Wool"	G. Love and Special Sauce
"Thank you"	Dido

Twenty-Two

Unsolicited Advice aka Lessons Learned

1. You must be clear and direct about what you want because everyone has their own objectives, and they won't always be upfront about them.
2. When you are dating in your 30's, you need to look your date in their eyes and ask, "Are you currently married?"
3. You are responsible for creating your own fun.
4. Someone else's broken heart was way too much for me to carry and that might be true for you too.
5. Absolutely no decisions should be based on profile pictures alone. You need to meet, face to face, as soon as possible.
6. Never ever use the line, "I am happy to meet you anywhere!"
7. I found it is best not to be sober and starving on a date.
8. Beware of men with several B's in their name or username because they will only break your heart. (So, this one may not be widely applicable, but you might have your own letter that follows you around).
9. Don't move for the D, and yes, the D is exactly what you think it is.
10. Women who give you an up-and-down, toe-to-hair glance only cause trouble. If you spot them, steer clear.
11. "Never eat a peanut butter sandwich too fast." Unsolicited advice on the importance of patience and lubrication from Mike.